THE INTERNATIONAL MANAGER

THE INTERNATIONAL MANAGER

KEVIN BARHAM
and
DAVID OATES

First published in Great Britain by
Business Books Limited,
an imprint of Random Century Limited,
Random Century House, 20 Vauxhall Bridge Road,
London SW1V 2SA,
in association with The Economist Books Ltd.

Copyright © 1991 The Economist Books Ltd
Text copyright © 1991 Kevin Barham and David Oates
Charts and diagrams copyright © 1991 The Economist Books Ltd

All rights reserved

No part of this publication may be reproduced or used in any form or by any means –
graphic, electronic or mechanical including photocopying, recording, taping or
information storage or retrieval systems – without permission in writing from
The Economist Books Ltd.

British Library Cataloguing-in-Publication Data.
A catalogue record for this book is available from
The British Library.

ISBN 0-7126-4933-6

Printed and bound in Great Britain by
Butler & Tanner, Frome, Somerset.

Contents

Preface	6
1 The Advance of Internationalisation	9
International business priorities	
2 Changing Corporate Structures	24
3 Creating an International Spirit	43
4 What is an International Manager?	68
The key characteristics	
The international manager as leader	
Team membership	
Networking skills	
The life-long learner	
The Fiat experience	
The Price Waterhouse study	
5 Making Managers International	96
The international learning organisation	
International career planning	
An international career planning checklist	
6 Recruiting Internationally	123
7 Educating International Managers	138
8 Managing International Assignments	158
Appendices	
1. How to be More International	181
2. Profile of an International Manager	183
Index	189

Preface

Changes in the global business arena have stimulated unprecedented interest in international business. In the quest to exploit market opportunities around the globe, businesses are increasingly experimenting with new approaches and structures which cut across national boundaries. The free movement of resources of all kinds has become necessary to achieve maximum competitive advantage.

But if these experiments are to yield anything of lasting value, these businesses need to have people in place who can survive and even flourish in environments which are increasingly fluid and complex. The quest for this elusive new international manager has started in virtually every industrialised economy. Who is this person? What type of skills and abilities does he or she need? What are the best ways of developing cadres of such people? And finally, what is really meant by international business – what issues, competitive pressures and opportunities are covered by this amorphous term?

These were the pressing questions that international businesses were asking themselves in the late 1980s when the research group at Ashridge conducted its major research project "Management for the Future",[1] later published as *Shaping the Corporate Future*.[2] This gave an in-depth study of how some of Europe's leading businesses, including ICI, BMW and Electrolux, saw their environments as being reshaped by rapid and complex change. These businesses freely admitted that they had by no means found the answers – their only comfort was that many of their competitors were in exactly the same position.

With the start of a new decade, Ashridge Management Research Group (AMRG) extended its research to see what sort of solutions were beginning to emerge from the melting-pot. The first step in this scrutiny was to examine what published sources said about approaches to international management development. The findings of this search appeared in the report *Developing the International Manager*.[3] Armed with this information, AMRG then went directly to businesses in the USA, Japan and Europe to ascertain how they defined and developed international managers. The main results of a questionnaire which these international companies completed in 1989–90 are included in this book.

To add to this basic information, AMRG also organised two events in 1990. A think-tank held at Ashridge in February 1990 brought together senior personnel managers from Europe and North America to discuss the issues and problems of international management development. In April 1990, a study conference at Ashridge on the theme of "The International Manager" provided a forum for a wide range of researchers, consultants and management developers to present the findings of their current work and to meet other people with an interest in this area.

The questionnaire survey, the think-tank and the conference were followed by visits to selected companies in North America and Europe to investigate in greater depth their approach to developing managers for international business. In each of these organisations we talked to senior human resource managers and management development specialists. The interim results of the research were published in January 1991 in The Economist Intelligence Unit special report *The Quest for the International Manager*.[4] This report included 15 case studies compiled largely on the basis of the company visits.

In this book we have integrated those case studies and have added new material, partly based on further company visits. Where it serves to illuminate the issues further, we also describe the findings of other researchers into international management development.

In the course of the research, we modified many of the ideas with which we started. Our starting-point, when we carried out the questionnaire survey, was how organisations developed individuals as international managers and the issues involved in giving people international experience. As the research has moved on, and particularly in talking to the companies in the case studies, we have come to realise that international management development must play a wider and more fundamental role than simply developing individuals. It must be seen explicitly as a major route to creating the culture and developing the strategy of the international organisation.

We are extremely grateful to the companies that participated in our questionnaire survey in 1989–90 and in particular to the firms that allowed us to interview them about their approaches to international management development. They have enabled us to paint a new and detailed picture of the way in which companies in different industries and in different parts of the world are coming to grips with global realities.

We are also very grateful to Patrick Rich, chief executive of BOC, who provided information for the profile in Appendix 2. This vividly illustrates how one man has built a successful international career.

We would like in addition to thank our colleagues at Ashridge for their support, especially Edgar Wille, research associate in AMRG. Our thanks also go to Dr Nigel Holden of the University of Manchester Institute of Science and Technology who contributed the case study of NEC to the EIU report *The Quest for the International Manager*, from which extracts have been used in this book; and similarly to Naomi Stanford of Price Waterhouse whose paper to Ashridge's conference "The International Manager" formed the basis for a case study from which we have here taken extracts. We also greatly appreciate the help of Marion Devine who not only co-authored *The Quest for the International Manager* but also applied her excellent editorial skills to the draft of this book.

Kevin Barham
David Oates

References

1. K. Barham, J. Fraser and L. Heath, "Management for the Future", Ashridge Management Research Group and the Foundation for Management Education, 1988.
2. K. Barham and C. Rassam, *Shaping the Corporate Future*, Unwin Hyman, London, 1989.
3. K. Barham, *Developing the International Manager*, Ashridge Management Research Group, 1989.
4. *The Quest for the International Manager*, The Economist Intelligence Unit, Special Report No. 2098, January 1991.

CHAPTER 1

THE ADVANCE OF INTERNATIONALISATION

The past decade has seen an explosion of interest in international business. Internationalisation has stormed to the top of corporate agendas everywhere. As they turn their attention to the international scene, however, more and more companies are coming to realise that the international business environment of the 1990s and beyond is going to be fundamentally different. In this chapter, we look briefly at the reasons for this sea-change before examining, in Chapter 2, how these macro-trends are forcing leading companies to reshape and reposition their businesses. Most importantly, they are scrutinising their organisational structures in an effort to assess whether they can group their people and resources in new and more dynamic ways. From this process is emerging an impressive range of new corporate forms, many still at an embryonic stage, which are described and analysed in this book.

Internationalisation is an amorphous and slightly unwieldy term used to describe what is in reality a cluster of trends that is inexorably transforming the environment in which "international" and "domestic" companies operate (see Table 1.1 on page 10).[1]

The advent of the single European market is of course one of the most crucial sources of change. The possibility of a single European market was hardly contemplated ten years ago. Now, however, to quote *Fortune* magazine: "In a single, pivotal decade, Europe will transform itself from a pokey patchwork into a unified, fast-moving market place loaded with opportunities."[2] Although Europe will never be a totally homogeneous entity, trade barriers are rapidly disappearing, and so enabling quality, price and service to become the language of success in this large and fiercely competitive new market.

Table 1.1 **Factors causing companies to pay increased attention to international business**
(% of respondents ranking a factor's degree of relevance)

	High	Medium	Low
Single European market	52	27	15
Speed of market changes	52	27	8
Mergers/acquisitions	46	25	15
Foreign competition	42	31	19
Saturation of home market	29	27	33
Increased domestic competition	19	19	50
Senior management changes	10	19	54
Host government encouragement	6	23	58
Home government encouragement	4	17	60
Use of surplus capacity	2	21	60

Source: The Ashridge survey, 1989–90.

Not surprisingly, companies are asking themselves whether their product range and structures enable them to meet these exacting standards. If they are even to begin to address these issues, they urgently need to turn nationally oriented functional managers into pan-European product managers.

Meanwhile, other far-reaching events have been taking place. Fast on the heels of economic change within Europe came the dramatic social and political upheavals in Eastern Europe. The retreat from communism and German reunification have certainly complicated the creation of the single market. But, together with 1992, they have opened up a new concept of an even wider Europe. The advent of the new Europe was accompanied by the conclusion in 1989 of a North American free-trade agreement between the USA and Canada (Mexico will probably be included eventually). This will not only create a huge continental market but also, as in Europe, give companies in both countries the opportunity to become more powerful competitors on the global scene. In the Far East, too, Japan has been building its own informal sphere of influence as it integrates the fast-growing markets of the Pacific Basin countries into its own economic system.

Operating across national boundaries

Paradoxically, the very possibility of separate world trading blocks is leading to more integration across national boundaries. Firms are seeking insurance against protectionism by, for example, placing job-creation activities in countries in which they make significant sales, forming joint ventures and buying from local suppliers. This is what Japanese firms call "insiderisation" and what their competitors dub the "Trojan Horse" strategy.

The movement towards integration is also being driven by those companies which believe that moulding a collection of separate national markets into one home market will give them the scale and price structure necessary to compete in global markets. The Ashridge survey showed no shortage of companies anxious to develop global strategies. A British firm, for instance, said that it had to become global because it operates in a market in which it will become increasingly difficult to sustain profitability unless it is operating on a global scale. A Swedish company cited its motto: "The world is our work site." Other companies indicated that they were taking a "triad" approach to international business, targeting the three major markets of Europe, North America and Japan.

The swing towards globalisation is reflected in the activities of those companies which service global production. Booz Allen & Hamilton, the major US consultancy, spent several years pursuing a policy of spreading its presence throughout the world in the belief that globalisation would eventually become the paramount issue for most of its clients. At times, the strategy led to substantial investment in parts of the world that showed little promise of a quick return. Now, as the realisation has spread among its client firms that international expansion is the only real guarantee of survival, the consultancy is starting to reap the rewards. John Harris, Booz Allen's European president, summarises this. "Most of the companies we work for, even those in the Asia–Pacific region, are worried about world markets. They're worried about scale; they're worried about how they operate effectively in different cultures and how they use local people in companies that are owned in a different country."[3]

In order to respond to these concerns, Booz Allen has assembled international teams of consultants. "The pan-European approach means doing European work with European teams," explains Harris. "We think that is the best way to serve clients who operate throughout Europe and the rest of the world. This is a major change because, historically, everyone consulting in Europe has been organised on a local basis."

The legal profession, by tradition relatively insular and inward-looking, is similarly responding to the swing to internationalism. Particularly enticing opportunities exist for Britain's top law firms, which unlike their continental rivals have long seen an advantage in size. Of the 20 largest practices in Europe, 18 are British and 2 are Dutch. The largest of all is Clifford Chance, based in London, which has almost 1,000 lawyers and operations throughout Europe, the Middle East, North America and Asia. Geoffrey Howe, Clifford Chance's managing partner, comments:

> "We are starting to get companies which realise that if they want to operate in Europe, they need to deal with a law firm which understands the way the company works and its own national law, yet which can translate all that into the local context of another country. This is especially the case for companies which are trying to sell highly complex products into international markets."

Clifford Chance has come to realise that success in international markets hinges on building a truly pan-European network. This is not the same thing as being a City-based business with offices throughout Europe, which is how the company saw itself two years ago before undertaking a strategic review of its operations.

> "We consider that we have an opportunity to do what no one has ever done, or tried to do. We are aiming to build a law firm that is truly European; the legal service offered by our offices in Europe must be that of a leading law firm in its own right in the relevant country. That means that we have to have local lawyers and we have to grow and develop our operations in the major European centres. In doing this, we believe we will be able to provide a better service to a client by having our own local presence instead of relying on partnerships with other practices."

Creating this kind of international network, Clifford Chance believes, will result in a winning combination of in-depth local knowledge and product specialisation, with both international and national clients being served equally well. Internationally experienced lawyers can work with local lawyers on cross-border transactions; product specialists can work with local lawyers to ensure clients receive a service entirely suited to their needs. Another advantage is that such an international network enables the firm to work in the most flexible way possible, especially in dealing with the minefield of different national regulatory systems currently existing within Europe.

It is no exaggeration to conclude that the global aspirations of companies everywhere constitute a major force that is reshaping the world economy. Walter Wriston, former chief executive of Citicorp, sums up the revolution that is taking place when he says that "national economies can no longer be understood – or operated within – unless you understand them in connection with all other economies. There are no islands any more."[4] No firm can ignore the international dimension. Even the most domestically oriented business is likely to find that it is operating in somebody else's international market. Unfortunately, as Kenichi Ohmae, one of the most perceptive observers of the international scene, says in his book *The Borderless World*,[5] the changes that have brought about this "interlinked economy" have been so rapid that they have outrun the capacity of many companies and managers to make adjustments both to their organisational structures and to their underlying "nationalistic" assumptions and outlook.

Nevertheless, some companies are working hard to break down international barriers. Perhaps one of the best measures of internationalism was suggested by an internationally established North American firm in the Ashridge survey which said that it found the divide between "domestic" and "foreign" markets no longer a meaningful distinction, a view that was shared by several other respondents. Although a seemingly simple conclusion, it can sometimes take years of painful effort before a company truly succeeds in eradicating from among its employees their natural preoccupation with their own home market.

The pace of market change

The other major factor that is driving firms to give more attention to international business is the speed of market change. A number of interrelated forces are propelling this acceleration.

Communications

Perhaps the most fundamental trend is the globalisation of communications. The allied forces of computers and telecommunications ("compunications") are bringing about the "annihilation of space", to use Daniel Bell's expression.[6] According to John Naisbitt and Patricia Aburdene, best-selling authors of *Megatrends 2000*:

> "We are laying the foundations for an international information highway system. In telecommunications we are moving to a single worldwide information network, just as economically we are becoming one global marketplace. We are moving toward the capability to communicate anything to anyone anywhere, by any form – voice, data, text or image – at the speed of light."[7]

International finance

The rapid pace of international financial transaction increasingly poses new problems. The burgeoning international currency market has become a largely speculative one whose roller-coaster movements can overnight undermine the best-laid plans of any company. One expert on international finance has suggested that: "If business is a war without bullets, then that war is increasingly fought out on a floating battlefield. Imagine an army that struggles mightily to take a hill, only to find that the hill has turned into a valley overnight, and the plain on which the enemy had been beaten is now the high ground."[8]

The management guru, Peter Drucker, believes that the problems of currency management mean a fundamental change of mind-set for many organisations. They must regard themselves, he says, as financial institutions as well as makers of products and services.[9] In other words, the management of currency must move to the centre of strategy-making and not be left as an afterthought to decision-making.

Product cycles

One of the most significant factors driving the ever faster rate of change is the desire of companies to outpace their rivals in developing new products and delivering them to the market place. Under the impact of "time-based competition", product life cycles are accelerating and becoming ever shorter.

Much of this competitive pressure is, of course, due to the decided superiority that Japanese firms enjoy in new product development. One estimate, for example, suggests that whereas Western firms take 16–20 days over the sales, order and distribution cycle for a car, Japanese firms take 6–8 days. While Western firms take 14–30 days to manufacture a vehicle, Japanese firms take 2–4 days. And while Western companies spend 4–6 years on new vehicle design and introduction, their Japanese competitors accomplish it in 2½–3 years.[10]

The Japanese approach is based on simultaneous (or parallel) engineering. Instead of a slow, sequential process in which responsibility for a new product is passed from design to production and on to marketing, the simultaneous approach brings people from all the functional areas together in a multi-disciplinary project team. This approach identifies problems earlier, speeds up decision-making, resolves interdepartmental conflicts and reduces delays. In a desperate bid to keep abreast of their Japanese competitors, Western firms are being forced to adopt similar approaches. This means that as the world economy is becoming more integrated, so too are the internal operations of firms becoming more interdependent. The challenge is to get different functions such as research and development, engineering, production, marketing and distribution working much more closely together than in the past, replacing rivalry with collaboration.

The pace of change becomes ever faster. Stanley Davis, author of *2001 Management*,[11] believes that consumers will increasingly demand products that can be delivered in their own time and space. He challenges firms to consider how they might create "instantaneous products and services" that can be delivered "within the blink of an eye of their conception". Few firms may yet be capable of such a *tour de force*, but, as Davis says, thinking about how this might be done could speed up even the slowest firm.

Perhaps the most daunting impact of this much increased rate of change is that many firms now "going international" for the first time do not have the option of a slow, cautious "let's test the water gradually" approach. The luxury of a low-risk, slow learning process simply no longer exists. Some of the firms in the Ashridge survey that were relatively new to the international scene pointed out some of the difficulties of entering and opening up new markets. They face such problems as lack of detailed market knowledge, unfamiliarity with different distribution channels and having to cope with different product standards. In the end, however, as one firm said: "It all depends on our own single-mindedness and determination."

These, then, are the trends and events that are transforming the international business scene; new economic alignments around the world; a move towards market integration and transnational activities; and rapid market change, stemming in particular from ever shorter product cycles. How should companies be responding to these challenges? What sort of strategies do they need to have in place in order to ensure that progress, not panic, is their managers' experience of the 1990s?

INTERNATIONAL BUSINESS PRIORITIES

The Ashridge survey attempted to answer these questions by asking companies to describe in their own terms the range of issues and competitive pressures that they are currently encountering. Overall, these companies highlighted four major priorities: the need to develop more sophisticated marketing strategies; establish new business alliances; develop coherent international human resource strategies; and create corporate structures that can cope with an increasingly complex international environment.

Responding to increased competition

Faced with accelerating change, it is not surprising that many firms in the survey expected greater competition over the next five years and expressed concern about their ability to retain and expand their market share. Companies in the more mature industry sectors voiced worries about slower growth in their markets. In some industries, too, concentration is leading to fewer but bigger and more power competitors. High-tech sectors, such as the computer industry, foresee greater competition from Japan and keener competition for a place in the post-1992 European market. Sectors as different as the hotel and telecommunications industries were worried about the speed of change in their international market places and spoke of great pressures on their ability to maintain a high rate of growth.

Not surprisingly, therefore, virtually every firm said that marketing, customers and developing a customer-orientation were major priorities for the future. Some well-established firms declared that they were becoming more selective in their choice of markets, both in geographical and product/service terms, in search of the most profitable segments. Some are focusing on Europe: "adapting to the reality of 1992", as one company put it. Some are also shifting attention to fast-growing markets in Asia and the Pacific region. One US firm spoke in particular of its desire to change the perception that it is a US-based company.

Many firms are aware of the need to keep pace with faster-moving, often contradictory trends (such as simultaneous globalisation in some market sectors and fragmentation in others), and to identify changing life values, new consumer habits and emerging customer attitudes. Some are also highly aware of the need to respond positively to growing popular concern about both the global and local environments. Industries like the chemical sector believe that this will have major implications for their ability to obtain raw materials.

More and more companies realise that service and know-how constitute an increasingly important part of their competitive edge. With products becoming increasingly similar and technological advances offering only fleeting advantage in many industries, service will become ever more important. One estimate suggests than nine out of ten managers in the USA and Europe will be suppliers of services rather than goods by 2000.[12] Maintaining consistently high-quality service is difficult enough in the domestic market, but managers will have to understand how to deliver it in international markets too.

Gunnila Masreliez-Steen, president of Kontura consulting group in Sweden and keynote speaker at Ashridge's conference on "The International Manager" in April 1990, says:

> "When you sell a product, the knowledgeable buyer will know how to evaluate the functions of the product for sale. When you sell know-how and service, you have already moved into the area of software. This is much harder to evaluate in an international context. It depends much more on our ability to make contact and build relationships over borders."[13]

Strategic alliances

For firms entering new markets, a special challenge is to find new business partnerships and build new relationships. As one firm in the Ashridge survey perceptively pointed out, developing joint ventures and close co-operation with companies in other countries means accepting that such co-operation must change the way that a firm looks at its own tasks and activities.

According to Kenichi Ohmae, "corporate leaders are beginning to learn what the leaders of nations have always known: in a complex, uncertain world filled with dangerous opponents, it is best not to go it alone." Many companies are now forming strategic alliances with companies in other countries to gain access to new markets and technology, to achieve global spread or to share the costs of research and development. These alliances go beyond the limited scope of the traditional joint venture in that they are central to the fundamental, long-term interests of the partners. Companies may often establish such alliances with firms with whom they are competing in other markets and products. For instance, General Electric deals with companies that are "competitors in the morning, customers at lunch, and joint venture partners in the afternoon".

Rosabeth Moss Kanter has called the process "becoming PALs – pooling, allying and linking across companies".[14] Such alliances can overnight transform the competitive configuration of an industry. The Volvo-Renault pact announced in February 1990 would make the combined entity into the fourth largest car manufacturer in the world after General Motors, Ford and Toyota. Volvo's chairman, Pehr Gyllenhammar, has called the pact "a new corporate model" which will replace "the old, hierarchical way" of running companies.[15]

The airline industry is a salient example of strategic alliances becoming vital to future viability. In an increasingly liberalised and competitive climate, many airlines are seeking closer links with each other to gain economies of scale and to fight off takeover bids. Lufthansa, for example, has moved closer to forming a new German airline, incorporating former East Germany's Interflug, and has forged closer links with Air France. Singapore Airways has set up a trilateral relationship with Delta Airlines of the USA and Swissair. British Airways and KLM Royal Dutch Airlines attempted to set up a joint venture with Sabena of Belgium (although the attempt ran into problems and had to be called off). Alitalia has established commercial agreements with Iberia of Spain and US Air.

In 1990 SAS cemented existing co-operation agreements by forming a strategic alliance with three other airlines: Austrian Airlines, Finnair and Swissair. The partnership, described as "a teaming of equal partners in a European quality alliance", together employs 80,000 people and deploys 250 aircraft which carried 30 million passengers in 1989. SAS and Swissair have consolidated their alliance by swapping each other's shares.

The alliance aims to work together on customer service, marketing and sales and technical work. The airlines are also planning to co-ordinate schedules to provide better connections within Europe and abroad, and are considering a new joint cargo centre in Vienna as well as check-in collaboration at various airports. One benefit is that the new entity will also have more purchasing power with aircraft manufacturers.

SAS is seeking further integration to add to its customer appeal by connecting hotels with airlines to provide an easier and more reliable service. Already at some SAS hotels it is possible to check in luggage and get a flight seat reservation at the hotel. In future technical advances will make it possible to check in to the hotel while still in the air and, once at the hotel, to use the company's Club EuroClass card to open the door to the hotel room.

Jan Carlzon, SAS president, has commented: "SAS has become a global travel service which is something very different from an airline that also happens to own a few hotels." SAS believes that if its alliances are to work effectively in delivering a global travel service, people in the company must know about the other companies and about the cultural differences involved in working with them. This is particularly important from the point of view of providing customer service in the global travel firm. SAS therefore subscribes to the need to "glocalise". To create a global travel company, it believes it is necessary for people to have a global view. At the same time SAS believes it is necessary to adapt marketing to local perceptions and to make service responsive to different local needs.

Furthermore, as SAS internationalises and connects its systems to those of its alliance partners, people must be trained to communicate and to work more effectively together. It is not only top management who have to understand and relate to the other organisations. Such understanding must be more widely spread throughout the firm. For example, no SAS employee should find it disorienting to sell an air ticket for Swissair, a former rival, rather than an SAS one if it is to the advantage of the customer.

International human resource management

The degree of success that companies achieve in their globalisation policies will depend greatly on their approach to international human resource management (HRM). Among the companies which took part in the Ashridge survey, international HRM issues, including management development, vie with customers, alliances and organisation design as top priorities for the future.

Major HRM concerns include:

- identifying and retaining highly qualified people;
- ensuring sufficient quality and quantity of management at the appropriate time;
- ensuring management succession;
- sustaining and improving performance at all levels in all areas of business;
- increasing the depth of talent in the organisation;
- making sure that people have the technical and managerial skills to compete;

- making the management competences and culture that are required sufficiently clear to people;
- total quality management and changing people's attitudes to quality;
- establishing training as part of the management culture;
- gaining top management and line management interest in human resource development;
- linking HRM to strategic objectives.

Addressing all these issues is a major challenge in a purely domestic setting. As one company said, the challenge will lie in ensuring that human resource management "adequately responds to new international market orientations".

International recruitment – "attracting people with international experience and vision", as one respondent described it – is accordingly a growing concern. A frequently noted anxiety among the European firms in the survey centred on ensuring an adequate supply of high-calibre staff and on attracting and retaining the best people internationally.

The demographic time-bomb and the drive towards internationalism among firms are combining to make the market for talent a much more international one. Companies will therefore have to ensure that the reward packages they offer are internationally competitive. UK firms may face particular problems in this respect. One British company noted that a major problem in the future would be the fact that senior managers in overseas subsidiaries receive higher remuneration than its UK-based executives.

Firms are already encountering shortages of the high-quality people they require. One UK firm bent on international expansion was worried that its growth is already stretching its systems and its management resources. It pointed in particular to a lack of competent international functional specialists. An American firm disconsolately concluded, "there are few managers with a true international perspective". Other firms are having difficulties releasing experienced people from existing operations in order to resource and lead new international ventures. These are all indications that a dearth of internationally skilled people may be an important constraint on firms' international ambitions and that the development of the international manager will be an important priority for the future.

The need for radical restructuring

The purpose of this chapter has been to show that the internationalisation of business is not merely a challenge waiting around the corner. It is already here, and any company with ambitions of global expansion can ill afford to ignore its implications. Internationally advanced companies have recognised for some time that the distinctions between domestic and export markets are fast crumbling in virtually every part of the world. Almost any kind of domestic business is seeing, or soon will see, its markets invaded by foreign players. These companies may still think of themselves as national operations, yet are nonetheless directly experiencing the impact of internationalisation. They are being forced to learn the lesson that if they will not go to the international market, it will come to them.

Those companies that have read the writing on the wall and are making concerted efforts to become truly international do not underestimate the size of the challenge. They are stepping into the unknown. The old cosy definitions of international business are now defunct; terms like "exporting" and "importing", "domestic" and "overseas" are increasingly irrelevant. Old rules encourage a mind-set that is in danger of being insular and limited. The companies interviewed by Ashridge were well aware that they are starting with a largely blank page. Throughout this book, we chart their quest for a new language; a fresh way of perceiving their environments; more complex and fluid organisational structures; new strategies and new leadership styles.

References

1 The research on which this book is based consisted of a questionnaire survey of 48 companies carried out by Ashridge Management Research Group in 1989-90 and interviews with companies in the spring and summer of 1990, subsequently augmented by interviews in early 1991 (see Introduction). Hereafter, references to the "survey" refer specifically to findings from the questionnaire survey.
2 S. Tully, "The coming boom in Europe", *Fortune*, April 10, 1989, pp. 28-36.

3 C. Rassam and D. Oates, *Management Consultancy: The Inside Story*, Mercury Books, London, 1991.
4 M. Magnet, "Stars of the 1980s cast their light", *Fortune*, July 3, 1989, pp. 36-49.
5 K. Ohmae, *The Borderless World: Power and Strategy in the Interlinked Economy*, Collins, London, 1990.
6 Quoted in P. Spooner, "Top managers – going global", *International Management Development Review*, 1989, pp. 77-79.
7 J. Naisbitt and P. Aburdene, *Megatrends 2000*, Sidgwick & Jackson, London, 1990.
8 G.J. Millman, "The floating battlefield: Corporate strategies in the currency wars", *Management Review*, April 1990, pp. 56-60.
9 P. Drucker, *The Frontiers of Management*, Heinemann, London, 1987.
10 G. Stalk and T.M. Hout, *Competing Against Time: How Time-based Competition is Reshaping Global Markets*, The Free Press, New York, 1990.
11 S.M. Davis, *2001 Management: Managing The Future Now*, Simon & Schuster, London, 1988.
12 P. Sadler, *Managerial Leadership in the Post-Industrial Society*, Gower, Aldershot, 1988.
13 G. Masreliez-Steen, "Building Bridges Between Culture, Service and Knowledge in a Cross-Cultural Context". Paper presented to the Ashridge Management Research Group conference "The International Manager", April 11-12, 1990.
14 R. Moss Kanter, *When Giants Learn to Dance*, Simon & Schuster, London, 1989.
15 L. Bruce, "Strained alliances", *International Management*, May 1990, pp. 28-34.

CHAPTER 2

CHANGING CORPORATE STRUCTURES

What kind of organisation is required to cope with an increasingly complex and faster-moving international environment? Many companies grappling with this question recognise the need to speed up decision-making by reducing bureaucracy and streamlining and flattening the organisation. Some are seeking more flexible structures, experimenting with taskforces and project teams. Some are decentralising to focus resources on particular markets, to push "ownership" further down the line, and to become generally more responsive to local markets.

At the same time, however, some firms identify almost the opposite of these trends as necessary to obtain the maximum benefit from pan-European and/or global opportunities. For example, one firm in the Ashridge survey said that it is seeking to co-ordinate and structure its activities so that its businesses work together as appropriate on all major issues such as strategy, products, services and resourcing. Another said that it is focusing on the integration of its worldwide businesses and acquisitions.

In an article for *Management Today*,[1] Tom Lester in describing this search by multinationals for an appropriate structure to meet the challenges of a single European market, embracing 440 million people in 21 countries, argues that they confront a problem that they are no nearer solving than the ancient Greeks.

> "The nub of the problem is the balance that has to be struck between central authority and local autonomy. If the pendulum swings too close to the centre, the corporate outposts are left floundering between an inappropriate strategy and local realities; too far in the other direction and the centre may be dragged towards the strongest

outposts with no capacity for radical moves when these become necessary. It is the classic dilemma that all empires experience..."

The widespread search for new organisation structures was underlined by a survey Lester carried out among more than 40 multinationals. Well over half of them had made significant organisational changes in the previous two years. "In 1990 alone BP, IBM, Hoechst and ICI all announced major restructuring programmes. All four appear to have pushed significant power out towards the periphery." Half of the companies in Lester's survey that had changed their structures had gone in this direction, while a quarter of them set out to strengthen central control. However, "even a superficial examination of the centralised/decentralised issues reveals that the complexities of modern multinational business demand that both styles are incorporated into the same structure, very often over the same issues."

These innovative companies apart, the majority of Western-based international companies probably continue to operate as traditional multinational firms. Such firms believe strongly in the merits of decentralisation and aim to respond to local conditions within an overall strategic framework set by head office. Their structure is likely to consist of a head office (or "corporate centre") based in the parent country and loose collections of scattered "subsidiaries" in countries abroad. Communication flows up and down the hierarchy through "chains of command" and the subsidiaries operate very much as separate companies. As one manager from such a firm comments: "Good international management boils down to good national management of devolved structures."

Such firms face a particular dilemma. They may wish to respond to local sensibilities by recruiting local managers and giving the jobs in subsidiaries to locals. This, however, can give powerful local managers the opportunity to create "baronies and fiefdoms" that prevent synergy between the various subsidiaries.

These firms are also bedevilled by "power hug". While overall strategy is formulated at the centre of the organisation, much of the information that is needed to monitor and adapt the strategy is situated in the organisation's outposts. Because information is a source of power, the people there naturally try to retain hold of it. The centre needs the information, but the outposts do not transmit it to head office. This is an increasingly serious handicap as the need to ensure free passage of information and to distribute ownership of strategy across the organisation becomes ever more pressing in an era of fast-moving world markets. Breaking down "power hug" is one of the most important tasks facing international firms in the future.

The transnational corporation

A radically different approach to this problem is suggested by Christopher Bartlett of Harvard Business School and Sumantra Ghoshal of INSEAD in their book *Managing Across Borders*.[2] The authors point out that most companies have traditionally built their international operations around one of three strategies. Companies like Philips and General Electric, they say, have pursued a multinational strategy that enables them to establish a strong local presence through responding to different national market requirements. The Japanese firms Kao and Matsushita on the other hand have operated as global companies, making themselves fiercely competitive by achieving substantial cost advantages from centralised global-scale operations. Ericsson and ITT have followed the third route and developed as international companies whose key strategic capability lies in exploiting parent company knowledge through worldwide diffusion and adaptation.

Bartlett and Ghoshal's central argument is that businesses can no longer afford to base their strategy on one focus. If companies are to cope with the complex international environment, they must have an equally complex and multi-faceted business strategy. Firms operating worldwide must pursue global, multinational and international strategies simultaneously. They must become what the authors call a transnational corporation, which has the following unique characteristics:

An integrated, networking structure

Traditionally, companies have subsidiaries which are either clearly dependent on the corporate centre (as in global companies) or strongly independent (as in multinational firms). Increasingly, however, these relationships are overly simple. International business now demands that every part of an organisation collaborates, shares information, solves problems and collectively implements strategy. An integrated network is needed to share decision-making and enable components, products, resources, information and people to flow freely between the transnational's interdependent units.

Decision-making through "co-option"

A major problem in any worldwide business is that managers in key positions are often limited by narrow perspectives and parochial interests, leading to substandard decision-making. In particularly complex, multi-tiered organisations, this problem is often exacerbated by conflicting interests and overlapping responsibilities. The commitment of every individual employee has to be won to the overall corporate agenda, a process that the authors call "co-option". To develop such a consensus, each individual must understand, share and "internalise" the company's purpose, values and key strategies.

Co-ordination

Traditionally companies have controlled their operations through one of the following three methods:

- companies like ITT depended on highly formalised and institutionalised control mechanisms;
- others like Kao favoured centralised decision-making; and
- businesses like Unilever took a very different tack and relied on socialisation to instil a common corporate culture and a shared perspective among its managers.

Bartlett and Ghoshal argue that a single method of control is insufficient – the very nature of the multi-dimensional transnational results in a dramatic expansion in the number of issues that need to be integrated. Consequently, all three processes are needed, and of the three, the authors believe that socialisation and co-option are by far the most effective means of co-ordination.

Innovation

Both global and multinational companies can stifle the flow of innovation throughout the organisation. On the one hand, independent subsidiaries within multinationals can sometimes block new ideas and innovations developed at the corporate centre. On the other, a centralised global company may be unable to introduce local innovations because of unmotivated or incapable local managers. Instead of encouraging local innovations or imposing ideas from the centre, the transnational allocates worldwide product responsibilities to different national subsidiaries according to their relative skills and strengths. This not only taps the particular expertise of the business unit but also confirms its identity in the company's global operations. This approach constitutes the transnational's most vital strength; its ability to facilitate organisational learning by fostering a flow of intelligence, ideas and knowledge around the organisation.

The transnational organisation makes difficult demands, however. Much more effort has to be put into welding the organisation together. Travel increases exponentially and a high price has to be paid in terms of exhaustion. The transnational is also an "untidy", multi-dimensional affair; often it is not clear where decisions are made. Nor does it necessarily solve the problems of "power hug". As one manager from an aspiring transnational company in the Ashridge research points out: "Political issues can get out of hand sometimes. It is easier with fiefdoms because you know where the politicians are."

How can a company turn itself into a transnational? Surprisingly, Bartlett and Ghoshal do not believe that the most important first step is to change formal structures and reporting relationships – of much more importance is the need to change the attitudes and perceptions of managers and employees. Companies, they say, should promote a clear, shared understanding of their mission and objectives, an understanding that results in a "matrix in the mind".

Creating the transnational company – Electrolux
Sweden's Electrolux, the world's largest manufacturer of household appliances, is believed by some observers to epitomise the emerging transnational company. A comparative newcomer to the world of multinationals, Electrolux has pursued a remarkable policy of acquisition over the past few years, showing great skill in turning around ailing companies and linking them to the Electrolux family without robbing them of their individuality. The acquisitions have included

Zanussi in Italy, White Consolidated in the USA and Tricity and Bendix in the UK. Electrolux now employs nearly 150,000 people worldwide, of whom 20 per cent are in Sweden, and comprises some 500 operating companies in 46 countries. Nearly 83 per cent of its sales are made abroad.

Although the household appliances operation accounts for more than 50 per cent of its turnover and largely shapes the evolution of the organisation, the company also has interests in chain-saws, garden appliances, car seat-belts, professional catering equipment, aluminium smelting, commercial cleaning and laundry services, farm machinery, industrial shelving and sewing machines. Despite this diversity, the company does not see itself as a conglomerate and has sought to create a portfolio which offers possibilities for developing synergies.

As Electrolux switches its focus from growth by acquisition to internally generated growth, its approach to managing its widely dispersed organisation is in transition, involving changes in both strategy and structure. Under the leadership of its president and chief executive, Anders Scharp, Electrolux has globalised several of its product lines, including household appliances (known as "white goods" in the trade), in an attempt to achieve cost leadership by exploiting economies of scale in production, particularly by using common components for different products.

Electrolux had previously tailored finished products to local markets (and will continue to do so where necessary), but it believes that the convergence of consumer taste and the emergence of "global lifestyles" is eroding international boundaries. For example, groups of consumers in New York, Stockholm and Milan now have more similarities than consumers in Manhattan and the Bronx within New York itself. This trend offers further opportunities for Electrolux to globalise its products.

The company has long pursued a policy of decentralisation; so much so that it used to talk about itself as a collection of independent "villages". Electrolux now wants to integrate these into interdependent but flexible "networks", with product development, manufacturing and supply all spanning international borders. A series of articles in the *Financial Times* in 1989 showed how the company is evolving a seemingly complex, multi-dimensional structure that it hopes will provide the necessary flexibility.[3]

The white goods business is pursuing a "multi-centred" approach whereby it is pushing "centre" functions out to the countries, leaving head office to concentrate on managing key competitive factors and to act as coach and co-ordinator. In its three product sectors ("cold", "hot", "wet"), each of which is co-ordinated by a product area manager, Electrolux has created small, nationally based product development/production units which have global responsibility for certain products. The UK, for example, is not only a national unit, but is also responsible for microwave ovens worldwide, while Italy is globally responsible for washing machines.

These units maintain customer–supplier relationships with Electrolux's national marketing and sales companies which are themselves co-ordinated by a small central marketing staff. The scale and complexity of the white goods business means that Electrolux must retain separate country managers to oversee all units, both production and marketing, within their territory. These individuals are also responsible for dealing with large retail customers and trade unions.

Electrolux has also experimented with drawing staff from different units into multi-disciplinary taskforces responsible for product design and development. For example, the design of a new refrigerator was carried out in Italy; engineering and initial production took place in Finland with assistance from Sweden; marketing advice came from the UK; and the product, if successful, may be manufactured in the USA. As one product area manager said: "We not only want to create common projects that span several units, but a process that allows responsibility to be transferred between them as the projects develop."

In place of the "traditional, military-style" hierarchical organisation with its rigid boss–subordinate relationships and chains of command, therefore, Electrolux is striving for interactive global networks with multiple channels of communication. This highly integrated cross-border structure, is, according to Leif Johansson, the head of the white goods business, "a quite impossible organisation, but the only one that will work".

Because Electrolux wants to avoid creating bureaucracy at all costs, the success of the strategy depends on constant and open communication, the willingness of senior managers to travel a great deal and an ability to tolerate ambiguity. It also rests critically on the organisation's ability to promote mutual understanding, empathy and trust across borders.

Kurt Vikersjö, Electrolux's executive development manager, described the challenges to the Ashridge researchers.

> "We do not rely too much on structure. We have strict financial control which is a necessary part of our decentralisation, but otherwise we do not overemphasise structuring. This means we communicate and communicate, our people travel a tremendous amount, and this is the only way of making sure that people understand you and that you understand them."

A cross-border mind-set

We found that the continuation of Electrolux's informal and non-hierarchical style of organisation has been a challenge in the face of its growing internationalisation and diversification. It continues to set its face against heavy bureaucracy and does not want to see the power of central staff grow. Neither does it believe in implementing strategy by decree. As Vikersjö says, it is all very well for head office to make decisions about positioning brands, but if the local managers do not agree (because they have too parochial a view), they can hamper the implementation of global strategy.

> "You must have a deep understanding globally because everybody is now a part of a cross-border network. You have to define the global strategies in order to decentralise and have the courage to make the necessary decisions, which will always involve some conflict. At the same time you have to develop ownership so that people really want to pursue the strategy."

This entails a degree of culture shock. "People have to change their attitude from being a good Dutch manager, or Italian manager, or Swedish manager, to being a good brand manager or a good cross-border manager." Although some Electrolux managers have been resistant to change, Vikersjö has generally been greatly impressed by how readily some of them have been able to adapt.

> "In the international taskforces with, for example, Italians, Americans and Swedes, it has been surprisingly easy to produce concrete results. Of course there is turbulence in the beginning, but then they achieve a result and success feeds on success. Once they have succeeded, they think this new international environment is very interesting. They have experienced a cultural 'shock' which is difficult but is a reality they have to go through."

Commitment is a vital factor in making such international teams work for Electrolux. Even the inevitable conflicts can be harnessed to give ultimate strength to the whole. Developing the cross-border mind-set in all the company's managers and specialists is, however, a slow process and will not happen overnight. In Vikersjö's view, it is a "long, maturing process".

Ultimately, what Electrolux is moving towards is a global community of understanding. "If we try to implement bureaucracy," says Vikersjö, "it will not work because it is against our culture. Instead we must develop a strong consciousness." This involves a "cultural amalgamation", rather than a structural or bureaucratically enforced management style.

The changes in Electrolux are the fruit of some years of experimentation with more fluid organisational structures. Some companies are, in contrast, attempting to become transnationals through a series of bold and drastic structural changes. IBM has long been regarded as the very model of a mature multinational, but according to Christopher Lorenz, writing in the *Financial Times*,[4] it was only at the end of 1990 that the computer giant positioned itself to become "a full member of a select band of pioneering 'transnational' manufacturers which includes two of its arch rivals, Hewlett-Packard and NCR". The move which appears to be catapulting IBM to transnational status was that of shifting the headquarters of one of its six main product divisions from the USA to Britain. The decision set in motion the transfer of 120 executives from IBM's $10 billion-plus communications systems business in New York to London in 1991.

The heterarchy

A related and equally radical new theory has emerged from Sweden, a country whose leading businesses have been grappling with the challenge of international business for some time. Gunnar Hedlund and Dag Rolander of the Stockholm School of Economics argue that a new form of organisation called the "heterarchy", as opposed to the hierarchy, is needed for international business.[5]

The heterarchy describes an organisation that is composed of "reciprocally interdependent and geographically dispersed centres, which are held together by shared strategies, norms and information" (echoing Bartlett and Ghoshal's concept of co-option). The heterarchy has many kinds of centres, allocating headquarter functions to wherever is most appropriate in the world, and allowing overseas "subsidiaries" to undertake strategic and global roles for the whole company. No dimension, whether product, function or country, reigns permanently supreme. The heterarchy is flexible and takes into account shifts in the business environment; "at a certain moment, global product management is important; next year perhaps integration of total R&D is paramount", explain Hedlund and Rolander.

Like the transnational, the heterarchy uses a wide range of approaches to control and co-ordinate its operations: it may use arm's-length arrangements such as joint ventures for some tasks or it may insist on "managing by decree" in others. Whatever method it uses, the heterarchy always aims to find the best means to achieve the task rather than adhering to a standardised format. Integration occurs through "normative means" such as corporate culture, shared values and managerial style.

Hedlund and Rolander use the analogy of the hologram to illustrate the nature of the organisation. Information about the whole is stored in every part of the company. The firm's basic strategy, its guiding principles of conduct, and access to detailed information are widely shared throughout the organisation. It becomes "a learning organisation" that empowers all employees to participate in and develop strategy. The authors say that the new organisation represents the "firm as a brain" approach as opposed to the traditional "brain of the firm" attitude where all strategy and innovation emanates from the top. The whole organisation is expected to think, and to act directly on thinking. The ethos of the heterarchy is one of moving forward through continuing experimentation.

While some of the companies that Ashridge interviewed are indeed starting to use the word "transnational", very few have added "heterarchy" to their management vocabulary. Discussions with international companies convinced the Ashridge team that it is premature to predict one archetypal organisation for the future. International companies are exploring a myriad different approaches, presenting a highly varied picture of strategic evolution. Each is grappling with a different context and raft of challenges – each of them perceive themselves to be at only the starting-point of their own definition of internationalism.

The mix of company models

Many of the companies we spoke to are still struggling for the right balance between strategic co-ordination and direction and decentralisation and autonomy. We found that some are trying to resolve this issue by introducing matrix structures which mix geographical and product responsibilities, thereby breaking down some of the distinctions between central and national operations. During a panel discussion on "globesmanship" organised by The Conference Board in America, for example, Paul Oreffice, chairman of Dow Chemical, stressed the importance of the US group's matrix structure.

> "Everybody in Dow has three bosses: a geographic boss, a product boss and a functional boss. One out of the three sets your salary and is a little more important than the other two. The geographic boss takes precedence, because it is easier to find people who understand products and technologies than people who understand the social mores and ways of doing business in different countries. It is tremendously important to give the geographic part of our matrix the most important role."[6]

Rhône-Poulenc

State-owned Rhône-Poulenc of France, the world's eighth largest chemical group, also introduced a matrix structure in 1986. Rhône-Poulenc operates in more than 140 countries and employs 85,000 people. It is run by an executive committee of five directors, each of which is responsible for a business function, such as R&D or human resources, a geographic region and a business division.

The executive committee formulates specific strategic goals and communicates these to the national head of each country. This individual then collaborates with various strategic business units (SBUs) within the country in fine-tuning and implementing the strategy in specific local markets. There are around 60 SBUs, many of which have been running for little more than a year.

Edson Musa, a Brazilian and the only non-French member of Rhône-Poulenc's executive team, believes that the SBUs have facilitated worldwide strategy analysis of the company's portfolio of activities. "Today we have a common language and group methodology," he stresses. The new organisation helps to set clear targets, establish a dialogue between operational managers and the executive committee, to delegate tasks and achieve greater accountability.

To outsiders the flow of authority through this form of organisation can appear unclear. For instance, who takes the ultimate decision about how strategy is implemented – executive committee members, country representatives or managers within the SBU? Jean-René Fourtou, Rhône-Poulenc's chief executive, is untroubled by this apparent confusion. "It is a living matrix. People must adapt the matrix for themselves," he told the journal *Management Today*.[7] He emphasises that the group wants to respect national cultures and ways of managing. Consensus is a strong value within the group. For example, Fourtou works with a committee that examines different aspects of Rhône-Poulenc's corporate culture and makes a point of saying to them, "if you will agree, I will agree as a matter of principle."

BOC

The company Edwards High Vacuum, a part of the BOC industrial gases group, is another which has introduced a matrix organisation to help it cope with the internationalisation of its business. To get closer to its overseas markets the company has been zoned into three regions – Europe, the USA and the Pacific. Managers operating in the zones report to their bosses in each region. But strategic product decisions are made at BOC's head office at Windlesham in England, where sales and marketing have been split into two units: systems and components. (Systems are complete solutions to a problem, such as a freeze-drying plant with all its ancillary support equipment, while components are things like vacuum pumps which may augment a system or be used on their own.) Danny Rosenkranz is the UK-based BOC director responsible for introducing the new structure.

> "The question was how do you link geography with product and in Edwards the problem was a lot of product, wide geography, wide technology. If you managed that in a pristine way, you'd go bankrupt; you'd have too many overheads. So you're really forced into some form of matrix management, which means a level of imperfection, if you like, in how clinical Edwards is."[8]

The London Business School (LBS) is so impressed with Edwards' solution that it uses it as a case study for its MBA programme. John Stopford of the LBS has said: "The human side – what they do to make their version of matrix management work – is important. They have built a team of people that are more interchangeable than most in British industry. There is real team building at Edwards; many companies talk about it but few achieve it."[9]

Unilever

Unilever, the world's second largest manufacturer of consumer goods, operates through a three-dimensional matrix structure based on product groups, territories and functions such as finance and personnel. In Europe, the product group axis has been the main reporting line since the 1960s when top-level product co-ordinators took over primacy from local country managers. In the three "overseas" regions (Africa and the Middle East, East Asia and Pacific, and Latin America and Central Asia), the main line is still through regional/country management.

Unilever, however, has been intensifying its focus on product rather than geography. In North America, where it previously held back from product co-ordination, the post of regional director has been eliminated and the Lever Brothers operating company split along product lines reporting directly to London. The focus on product has been given a further boost by the prospect of the single European market. The structure of Unilever's European business is being modified to make it more competitive post-1992. The aim is to be able to plan marketing in the framework of the single market without having to reinvent the wheel in different countries.

In January 1990, Unilever set up a new organisation called Lever Europe in a radical departure from its previous policy of decentralised marketing. The reorganisation was aimed at centralising responsibility for manufacturing and marketing its detergents in Europe. Business observers[10] have found the switch in strategy surprising in view of Unilever's long-cherished belief in decentralisation. Its previous approach freed local managers from central bureaucracy, allowing them to come up with innovative new products and marketing ideas.

This hands-off approach had much in its favour. But some analysts felt that it resulted in serious inefficiencies, particularly in the detergents area. For example, when competitors like Procter & Gamble and Colgate-Palmolive pushed into Europe in the late 1950s, they treated the continent as a greenfield site enabling them from the very beginning to launch standardised international brands that could be produced in one central location. This left Unilever, which was a hotch-potch of national brands built up by a series of acquisitions in the first half of the century, at a serious competitive disadvantage.

The centralisation that Unilever has now introduced to counteract this competitive disadvantage could, however, lead to new problems. The company might, for example, find itself out of touch with local consumers. If the brand they have known for many years suddenly changes, they could be alienated. Local managers, who may feel their personal contribution diminishing, could also be less motivated. Mike Dowdall (Unilever's detergents co-ordinator) insists, however, that in the long term the really good people will find themselves with "bigger and better rewarded jobs".

Unilever is fully aware, however, that many differences in consumer taste are likely to persist and that managing "limited diversity within a strategy" will not be easy.

Sir Michael Angus, Unilever's chairman, has no doubt that the company's new matrix structure has improved its decision-making process. He characterises decision-making at Unilever during the

1960s as two elephants making love. "It starts with a lot of beating about the bush. Then there is an enormous amount of activity at a very high level – after which nothing happens for 18 months."[11] Unilever had three principles in mind when it introduced "the much-maligned matrix structure". The first was the need for flexibility, the second the need to transfer good practice across countries and groups, and the third and in Sir Michael's view probably the most important, the encouragement of innovation from all possible sources because it is a mistake to assume that all innovation comes from the centre. "In my view, when the matrix structure fails, it is normally because people aren't trained to work within it. We are very fortunate in that we have a cadre of various nationalities that have been trained and developed to work in our sort of system."

Glaxo

Glaxo, the UK-based pharmaceuticals group, is another firm that has been striving to find the right organisational balance to accommodate its global strategy. It started life in New Zealand exporting dried milk to the UK. Many years later, it became British-based and eventually chose to concentrate its activities on the pharmaceuticals business. "What was missing through the greater part of Glaxo's history," writes Sir Paul Girolami,[12] "was a global strategy, with the appropriate international policies, organisation and management."

The organisation structure that has evolved at Glaxo is largely dictated by its concentration on a single business, which means "that all operating levels in its management structure and all its functions and activities, wherever they are located, can be identified directly with the group's strategies and polices". The group's organisational framework is characterised, according to Sir Paul, by an emphasis on leadership and quality of management rather than central authority and command; trust and partnership, rather than bureaucratic control. The centre, apart from defining the global strategy, leads this international complex, exercises functional control, sets international standards and co-ordinates the functions, operations and activities across national boundaries. "But the 'centre' does not have a strict geographical identity; it is a top management layer, international in composition and location."

Clifford Chance
The nature of the relationship between its London headquarters and its offices around the world is also changing at law firm Clifford Chance. The aim of the centre is now both to formulate broad strategic frameworks and to create an "organisational infrastructure" in which these strategies can be implemented. The firm is anxious for the various national practices to formulate their own business plans within the broader framework. This is achieved through annual business planning cycles within the various practices, which is overseen by managing partner Geoffrey Howe.

In the past, Clifford Chance's overseas offices were largely regarded as independent units and received little interference or support from London. Now, through such means as the annual planning cycles, the firm is trying to get all its operations to take more responsibility for strategy and business development. The firm's product groups, which are based in London, are beginning to think in international terms. "We are edging our way towards making our strategic planning a more integrated process, but there is still a little bit of dysfunction between the grand plan in London and some of the national operations."

BP
BP is a strong example of a company trying to free itself from the burden of head office. Within a week of taking over as chairman of the giant oil company in 1990, Robert Horton announced that more than 1,000 jobs would be cut from its massive headquarters in the City of London. With them went an elaborate hierarchical structure and some 70 committees, all supposedly needed to co-ordinate the global business. Horton felt that they stifled initiative and action in the operating units. A regional headquarters in Brussels is now being established to discourage head office interference in European issues.

TI
As most of these examples have shown, there is of course a strong relationship between a company's individual history and its current approach to structural change. When once domestically oriented companies spread abroad to take advantage of wider markets, the

shift from central control to devolved responsibility among overseas subsidiaries becomes inevitable. A case in point is TI Group, which, from 1986 to 1989, transformed itself from a UK-based manufacturer of engineering products, domestic appliances and cycles into a specialised international engineering company with 300 manufacturing and customer service facilities in 114 countries.

The rationale for the globalisation of the TI's activities was self-evident. The UK accounts for only 7 per cent of the world engineering market and is too small a base to generate a competitive position in the world. Equally important, according to Mark Radcliffe, a TI director,[13] is that the company's customers, particularly in vehicle manufacture and aerospace (both significant markets for TI), demand that their suppliers can operate where they manufacture.

TI has organised itself accordingly. All TI companies function under an international umbrella covering areas such as legal matters, taxation, treasury and financial accounting. The company has established an international database that is a crucial back-up for technicians working at John Crane International, a subsidiary that makes engineered seals. Seals may not be too hard to make, but in an essentially service activity technicians need to be able to supply exactly the right product to solve a customer's problems in different parts of the world.

Ericsson
Like other Swedish companies, Ericsson's small domestic market forced it very early in its history to go abroad in search of markets. One of its major strengths has been its ability to transfer its knowledge and expertise around the world and to adapt its technologies to local requirements. Ericsson also believes, however, that it should be able to tap into local expertise and exploit it globally. For example, Australia has been given a lead role in R&D because the Australian subsidiary has strong links with academic institutions. Information technology links the company to Stockholm's computer-aided design facilities.

Ericsson sees itself as having progressed from a traditional industrial company to a "knowledge company" that places greater emphasis on more comprehensive systems and know-how. Its products are also becoming more sophisticated and greater demands are being placed on special product knowledge.

SAS

SAS is another Scandinavian company that has recognised that the traditional hierarchic structure is outmoded when it comes to responding rapidly and directly to customers all over the world. In the 1980s, Jan Carlzon, its chairman, transformed SAS from an unprofitable aircraft and technology company into a successful "completely service-based enterprise". The company has been hailed as a model for service organisations in other countries.[14] One of the keys to this dramatic transformation was the recognition that service and front-line people are the success factors in a customer-oriented and market-driven era. This is encapsulated in Carlzon's notion that there are millions of "moments of truth" every year – the moments when customers come into contact with employees – which ultimately determine whether SAS succeeds or fails.

The old-fashioned hierarchical organisation structure is no way to capture these moments of truth and Carlzon has talked of inverting the pyramid so that "management" becomes a support for the vital front-line staff. Management is shifted from the executive suite to the operational level where everyone effectively becomes a manager of their own situation.

★ ★ ★ ★

The search for the right international strategies and structures continues. In this search, models like the "transnational corporation" and the "heterarchy" can help to clarify and stimulate thinking about the future of international organisations. Some companies warn against using them too narrowly and find them to be "labelling exercises" that fail to capture reality. It is certainly important to avoid becoming overly preoccupied with definitions and instead to follow the redoubtable advice of Humpty Dumpty in *Alice Through the Looking Glass*: "When I use a word, it means just what I choose it to mean ... the question is, which is to be master?" The aim of this book is to suggest ways of achieving "mastery" of business practice, not theory.

One of today's most perceptive and influential management experts, Rosabeth Moss Kanter, identifies the search for a new business mind-set as one of today's most important challenges. She points to the "triumph of process over structure" as a key indication of this change. "What is important," she says, "is not how responsibilities are divided but how people can pull together to pursue new opportunities."[15] In the international arena of the future, it is the ability of people from different countries and cultures to pull together that will be crucial for the success of the international firm.

References

1. T. Lester, "A structure for Europe", *Management Today*, January 1991, pp. 76-78.
2. C.A. Bartlett and S. Ghoshal, *Managing Across Borders*, Hutchinson Business Books, London, 1989.
3. C. Lorenz, series of articles on Electrolux in the *Financial Times*, June 19-30, 1989.
4. C. Lorenz, "IBM joins ranks of transnationals", *Financial Times*, December 10, 1990, p. 11.
5. G. Hedlund and D. Rolander, "Action in heterarchies – new approaches to managing the MNC" in *Managing the Global Firm*, C. A. Bartlett, Y. Doz and G. Hedlund (eds), Routledge, London & New York, 1990.
6. "Globesmanship", report of a panel discussion in *Across The Board*, the official publication of The Conference Board, January/February 1990, pp. 25-34.
7. G. Foster, "Rhône-Poulenc's chemical explosion", *Management Today*, April 1990, pp. 68-73.
8. "Managing a mini-conglomerate", *BOC Management Magazine*, no. 21, February 1991, pp. 20-29.
9. S. Holberton, "Esprit de corps: life-blood of the matrix", *Financial Times*, May 14, 1990, p. 13.
10. I. Fraser, "Now only the name's not the same", *Eurobusiness*, April 1990, pp. 22-25.
11. "Globesmanship", *op. cit.*
12. Sir Paul Girolami, "Worldly wise", *Management Today*, September 1990, p. 5.
13. T. Wilkinson, "TI's quest for a global culture", *The Independent*, August 21, 1990, p. 19.
14. K. Albrecht and R. Zemke, *Service America: Doing Business in the New Economy*, Dow Jones-Irwin, Homewood, Ill., 1985.
15. R. Moss Kanter, *When Giants Learn to Dance*, Simon & Schuster, London, 1989.

CHAPTER 3

CREATING AN INTERNATIONAL SPIRIT

The staff of an international company need a climate that encourages them to rise above nationalism, and beyond that, parochialism. An international spirit promotes co-operation across borders and the free flow of information and other resources around the organisation. It frees the corporate centre from having to monitor closely the way its business units are managed – if the company's values and mission have been internalised it can trust its people around the world to translate them into local action.

The change of mentality required to achieve this international spirit has been well summed up by Percy Barnevik, president and chief executive of ABB, the giant engineering group that grew out of the merger between Sweden's Asea and Switzerland's Brown Boveri. "Some people say that we have no home country – the truth is we have many home countries." Barnevik adds: "There is no parent around the traditional form; all operating companies are sisters. I sit in Zürich presiding over a 100-person headquarters. It will not get larger than this. We are creating a new concept of a truly European company."[1]

To gain a deeper understanding of how such a spirit can be developed, companies in the Ashridge survey were asked if they had established any ways of encouraging employees, including those in the parent country, to "think internationally" about their business activities. Some asserted that international thinking develops through the very task of conducting international business: regular international travel and frequent visits of senior management to subsidiaries, and the submission of strategic plans by overseas subsidiaries to the parent company all help to ensure that employees look beyond their own national contexts. "There is no choice but to think internationally," said one UK company. A Dutch company agreed: "With 50 per cent of our turnover abroad, employees receive daily exposure to 'international thinking'." "There is an international ingredient in most of our employees' job situations," said a Swedish firm, "such as dealing with international customers and suppliers and communicating with other companies in the group outside Sweden." Given time, indeed, there is no doubt that internationalism can become naturally embedded in company culture. As another company said: "It's now part of our culture. Your career depends on it."

Firms which are looking anew at the international scene, however, have found that getting people to think internationally is not a straightforward process. As one US firm admitted: "Part of our strategy is to strengthen our global market. However, this does not seem to be the encouragement needed for employees to 'think globally'. Only parts of the company are globally minded – we have a long way to go."

An important message from the firms that are striving to increase their international business is that internationalisation has to be an integral part of a firm's strategy and must be communicated intensively from the top downwards. They believe that there is insufficient time for an international outlook to grow organically through the normal course of day-to-day business. An international spirit will be sustained only through continuous attention and effort.

Why do companies need to give so much attention to developing an international spirit? The answer is that, despite the shrinking of the world described in Chapter 1, local culture continues to exert a major influence on the way that people think, behave and work together. Indeed, it seems that many aspects of globalisation trigger a counter-reaction that emphasises cultural differences. While a diversity of cultures can be a tremendous asset to an organisation, it can also pose considerable obstacles to the cohesiveness needed to compete internationally. It also adds to the forces that encourage the "power hug" that is the bane of the international firm.

The impact of national culture

There has been an increasing awareness over the past few years of the impact that national culture has on the way people manage and work together in organisations. One of the most influential researchers in this area is Geert Hofstede of the Institute for Research on Intercultural Co-operation in the Netherlands. Hofstede defines culture as the "collective programming of the mind" which distinguishes one group of people from another. His 40-country study (later extended to over 60 countries) of managers and employees in IBM[2] found highly significant differences in the work behaviour and attitudes of people from different countries.

Hofstede's study suggested that national culture explained more of the differences in work-related values than did an individual's position within the organisation, profession, age or gender. His findings suggest that cultures vary in four main dimensions: individualism versus collectivism; power distance; uncertainty avoidance; and masculinity versus femininity.

Individualism versus collectivism describes the nature of relationships within a society. This varies from countries where ties between individuals are very loose and everybody is expected to look after their own interests, to societies where ties between individuals are very close and everybody is expected to look after the interest of their own group and to hold the opinions and beliefs of that group. Wealthy countries like the UK, the Netherlands and the USA, are more individualistic than poor countries like Colombia, Pakistan and Taiwan.

Power distance measures the extent to which people in organisations accept the unequal distribution of power. Centralised authority and autocratic leadership are rooted in the mental programming, not just of people at the top, but also of those lower down in the organisation. "High" power distance countries include those in Africa, Asia and Latin America, although France, Belgium, Italy and Spain score fairly high too.

Uncertainty avoidance is how people cope with risk and ambiguous situations and how far they try to avoid these by providing career stability, establishing formal rules, relying on expert opinion, seeking absolute truths and rejecting deviant ideas and behaviour. Latin countries, Japan and Korea score highly here, while Germany, Austria and Switzerland score higher than other European countries.

Masculinity versus femininity is concerned with the extent to which a society emphasises the "masculine" values of assertiveness and the acquisition of money over the "feminine" values of relationships between people, helping others and quality of life. "Masculine" countries include Japan, Germany, Austria and Switzerland, Italy, the UK, the USA, Venezuela and Mexico. Countries at the feminine end of the spectrum include the Nordic countries and the Netherlands.

Hofstede does not suggest that all members of a cultural group will hold exactly the same values. Rather, the values are typical of that culture. The link is statistical, not absolute. He acknowledges that cultures shift over time but believes that most value changes are peripheral and do not touch the basic issues on which these four dimensions are founded.

If an organisation wants to create an international spirit, what factors does it need to take into account and how can it help people rise above these deep-seated cultural influences? How do some of the companies that Ashridge has talked to tackle this crucial issue?

Promoting core values

The companies told us that the most important step in creating an international spirit is to promote the core values that it wants its people to adhere to around the world. When an organisation is clear about its philosophy and values it provides a strong context in which people can plan and act. The simpler the message, as Pepsi-Cola International suggests, the easier this is to achieve.

Pepsi-Cola International

Dr John Fulkerson, director of human resources at Pepsi-Cola International, declares: "It cannot be 20 things. It must be just three or four things that people can remember so that they understand what's important in the culture and what are the things we really want to do."

An objective for Pepsi-Cola International is to build a corporate culture that encourages people to give each other "instant feedback" about how things might be done better. But Fulkerson recognises that different cultures require different approaches: "In the Far East, for example, you would still give instant feedback, but you might not do it except under careful closed door conditions so that the person is able to save face and so you don't embarrass or humiliate them. Whereas there are other cultures where you might pound the desk and get emotional about it."

On the whole, however, Fulkerson plays down any cultural differences: "We've allowed ourselves to say that borders drive what's going on. Yes, laws are different and business practices are different. But understanding how you manufacture aluminium cans is the same technology regardless of where you manufacture the can." Similarities, he suggests, are more important than differences, but the differences must be identified and discussed in order to understand that they are not important.

The important thing, in Fulkerson's view, is to help people to become more effective wherever in the world they operate. "What you get is a constant emphasis on making decisions, taking initiative, taking risks, surfacing new ideas, and supporting new initiatives. These constantly come across regardless of where you are because we know that change is the name of the game in everything that we do." Ultimately, cultural differences present no obstacles provided people remember the fundamental social and economic purposes of business: "The issue is how you can improve the lot of people in any given country."

General Electric

General Electric is another company that is trying to ensure that its business philosophy is spread among its personnel worldwide. Its watchwords are "speed, simplicity and self-confidence" and the prime aim for the 1990s is to become a "company without boundaries". It will recognise no distinctions between "domestic" and "foreign" operations; it wants to be as comfortable in Seoul and Budapest as in Connecticut and New York. It aims to remove the vertical boundaries of hierarchy and to knock down the internal walls which separate function from function and to "erase group labels such as 'salaried' or 'hourly' which get in the way of people working together". It also wants to join with suppliers to make them part of the single process of satisfying customers. It has accordingly pledged itself to manage across borders internally and externally, nationally and internationally.

Some 49,000 people, or 17 per cent of General Electric's 290,000 workforce, are employed outside the USA. The company earns 26 per cent of its revenues and 40 per cent of its operating profits from its international activities. Dr James Baughman, GE's manager of corporate management development, says: "Over the past decade, we have moved dramatically from being an American company to being a world player." But this does not mean that GE has ceased to be an "American flag" company. It does not see itself becoming a "stateless corporation"; it wants to "do business the French way in France and the Indonesian way in Indonesia, but with the GE flavour".

Ericsson

Ericsson, the Swedish telecommunications group, promotes its shared values through its educational and training programmes. These values include: a very professional business culture; respect for the individual and the importance of teamwork; perseverance and endurance. (The latter shows itself in Ericsson's persistence in trying to enter difficult markets such as Germany and the USA.)

The company is developing leadership programmes for junior and middle managers as part of a new worldwide career planning system. It wants to run the programmes on "a global basis", providing a common framework that brings together the different approaches that all the Ericsson businesses have developed in this area. A small international working group is devising a programme which can be run all over the world and translated locally. "At this level it is dependent on the different cultures," says Britt Reigo, Ericsson's senior vice-president for corporate human resources and organisation. "Many of these managers will never leave their own countries, but it is important for them to have the perspective of the basic qualities required of a leader in Ericsson."

Ericsson has no doubt that its core values can be translated around the world, but it knows full well that it cannot automatically assume that this will happen. It is coming to realise that much depends on the way that values are communicated and that their validity needs to be constantly monitored. Quality of communications has to be a major preoccupation of an international knowledge organisation such as this one. Knowledge workers cannot be motivated by orders; they must be inspired by challenges that arise from a well-communicated vision. Reigo feels that this is a major task for the company in the future: "We will save much more time if we can achieve this dialogue and get top managers to realise that what they say can take years to get through to the company."

Accor

One of the best examples of a firm that is trying to create an international corporate spirit is the fast-growing French hotels and restaurants group Accor. This company believes that corporate culture and values are the crucial glue that binds together a large international organisation and gives it unity. Volker Büring, Accor's vice-president for human resources, elaborates:

> "Accor is geographically dispersed with a flat hierarchy and few formal procedures. This means that the only way we can create a common base and feeling of solidarity and belonging is through emphasising our culture and values. Culture and values are much more important than systems; you can change the latter relatively easily, but to change the former is a fundamental task."

Creating such cohesion is no easy task in a group with 61,000 employees working for around 40 brands and speaking 20 different languages. But, says the company's annual report, "throughout the Accor worldwide community the same words come back again and again, no matter what the language. Together, these words form a sort of *lingua franca,* a universal language that expresses our shared spirit." Among these words are "success", "openness", "people", "customers" and "belonging".

Like many French companies Accor has chosen to articulate its values in the form of a written statement. In a small blue booklet called *Ethics & Management,* the company explains its core values relating to quality, profit, growth, innovation, training, participation, decentralisation and communication. It goes on to illustrate attitudes and behaviours that it wants to see in all its employees. The company's two co-chairmen explain in the foreword that the principal objective is "to show that certain values and morals enable people to open up and bloom and be autonomous. Finally, these ethics have shown that they have a role in motivating every person to succeed, both as an individual and as a team."

In many ways Accor is atypical of French companies. Volker Büring says that this is largely due to its chairmen, "real entrepreneurs, self-made men who are not concerned about status, hierarchy or formal education". Perhaps also in contrast to traditional French management styles, Accor encourages direct, face-to-face communication; "open doors" and humour. Of that trait, Büring says: "We believe you should have fun in your work – and we are having fun."

Perhaps because of its entrepreneurial roots, Accor does not feel that it needs to change its culture or values in the quest to become international: it believes its values are simple and comprehensive enough to be translated into different cultures. It recognises, however, that for this to happen successfully it must give employees the scope to translate these values into culturally appropriate actions and behaviours.

Communicating its culture around the world is therefore an important task. Training plays a vital role. Newly recruited or promoted managers come to Accor's training academy, based at Evry, France, for two days to learn about the company's culture and business activities. To assist the process, Accor has developed a board game called "strat Accor", which is based on a race across the world and through the group's trade names.

Unilever

It is clear that there are many ways that core values can be communicated to a company's international workforce, explicitly or implicitly. The important thing is, as Unilever warns, that corporate culture should not try to replace or challenge the local manager's identity. "Ideally," says Tony Vineall, Unilever's deputy director of personnel, responsible for worldwide management development, "managers should feel fully nationals of their own country, yet equally fully members of the corporate club." As the culture develops and matures it will do so by drawing on the cultures of all the countries where it operates.

As Vineall points out, corporate culture should not be strong in areas where it does not need to be strong and must not conflict with local culture. If, like Unilever, the culture is built slowly over time, it can be strong through its "weakness"; strong without needing to be oppressive or explicitly requiring people to subscribe to particular tenets. This is not to say that corporate culture and organisational climate do not need attention. "They are the air that multinational teams breathe," maintains Vineall. "If those climates are right, international teams will come together naturally and quickly."

Internationalism is ingrained in Unilever, which employs more than 300,000 people across the world in operating companies in more than 75 countries. David Jones, the group's head of training, maintains that an international spirit is virtually taken for granted. "It is axiomatic that management development is international because we are an international organisation. It is understood that it is the philosophy of the business."

Surprisingly for such a large organisation, informality is an important feature of the Unilever culture. The company does not maintain heavily documented systems. "It works by people knowing how things are done." Much, therefore, depends on informal relationships across the organisation. These links are formed from very early on in people's careers.

TI Group

Clearly, some companies are further advanced in establishing an international culture than others. For example, the sheer speed at which TI Group, the UK engineering firm, transformed itself from a predominantly UK organisation into an international group with facilities in 114 countries meant that management development took a back seat. The haste was necessary to retain the support of financial markets, but Chris Lewington, the group's chairman, admits that the new TI culture has not yet penetrated to any great depth. In a research paper prepared by Harvard Business School, he is quoted as saying: "I believe that until this culture really penetrates and managers think globally and operate globally, we will not truly realise the benefits of TI's global strategy."³

Clifford Chance

It is of course more difficult to achieve a common international culture in organisations that have not been in existence very long. Clifford Chance, Europe's largest law practice, was only formed in 1987 through a merger between two partnerships, Clifford-Turner and Coward Chance. In such a young organisation a corporate culture which promotes shared values and standards takes time to evolve. The process is not helped by the firm's wide geographical dispersion. The solution, Clifford Chance believes, is to work patiently to build up a corporate culture that promotes a small number of core values which will ensure that clients around the world receive a consistent picture of the firm. These values focus on building a "client-centred ethos" by making decisions which place the client's interest first, having pride in one's work, co-operating with colleagues, providing a high quality of service and enjoying cultural differences.

Geoffrey Howe, Clifford Chance's managing partner, believes that: "If you have not got any sense of history, you are missing an important part of your culture. Looking back and understanding how the firm has grown enables you to understand how the organisation reacts to certain situations and what sort of identity it has."

He believes that another way of developing a cohesive culture is through internal communication about the firm's strategy and ambitions. The company has therefore embarked on "a substantial communications project where we are developing much better media for our people. This enables us to explain to them what we are trying to do, how we are going to get there and how they fit into it all."

Monitoring values

Corporate values have to be maintained as well as established. Ericsson provides an instructive example of how an organisation can go about trying to ensure that its values continue to match the aspirations of the younger generation, a sector of the company that is increasingly significant.

As part of a development exercise, some senior Ericsson managers held discussions with groups of about eight young employees aged 22–30. The aim was to find out more about young people's values and how Ericsson was viewed as an employer. Are Ericsson's corporate values accepted? Are the things that young people value the same as those that management values? What do young people expect of an excellent employer and what are the most important steps the company can take to become one?

The exercise generated considerable enthusiasm among the Ericsson managers who took part. Altogether some 150 young people all over the world gave their views. Some national differences came to light, but, most importantly, a common concern emerged from the discussions to increase communication and dialogue all over the organisation. Britt Reigo, senior vice-president for corporate human resources and organisation, says the exercise provided an opportunity to test people's true opinions of the organisation and to help managers to adapt their attitudes.

Internationalising the composition of management

The way that a company staffs top management and fills key positions can provide a powerful message about its aims towards internationalisation. How far is the firm prepared to go in appointing people from different countries to top management positions? Does it want local nationals to run its subsidiaries or is it happy to see third-country nationals in charge of them? In other words, is it prepared to regard competence as more important than country of origin?

In oil company Shell, the top management board, known as the Group Managing Directors, shows an impressive richness of experience, all six having spent a good part of their careers overseas. Forbo, a Swiss wall-coverings firm, has directors from all the countries where it has factories, and by the process of foreign acquisition looks like becoming one of the first companies to have a truly global board. It holds board meetings in English, French or German. In the UK ICI has recently expanded membership of its board to include non-executive directors from Japan, the USA and Germany. But most British firms are slow to emulate such overt internationalism. A 1987 survey of 200 top UK companies by the Ambrosetti Consulting

Group found that 90 per cent of main board directors were still British. Nearly 80 per cent of the directors surveyed did not speak a second language. In a quarter of the companies surveyed, not one of the directors did so. American companies are not much better: only 12 per cent of the 1,000 largest companies in the USA have a non-American on their board of directors.

These companies have a long way to go to match Unilever's efforts to create an international top management team. It currently has five nationalities on its main board. The group's headquarters staff includes 30 different nationalities among its management and most of the company's senior staff have worked in two or three different countries. More than half of the top 450 jobs are held by people who are neither British nor Dutch. The company firmly believes that a significant proportion of the people running a business in a particular country should be nationals of that country. And if nationals of a country are to run a unit in an international business, they themselves should have worked outside their own country. It is also considered very important for them to have worked in head office.

Unilever's central office staff are expected to have had experience of working in other countries as well as a general perspective of different cultures "to avoid the trap of thinking too narrowly". David Jones, the company's head of training, refers to Christopher Bartlett's expression that managers need a "matrix in their mind". Jones adds: "But you don't get a matrix in your mind if you sit in a personal products company in one country for the whole of your life."

A growing number of firms are moving in the same direction as Unilever. The appointment of Volker Büring, a German national, to the top human resource job at French-based hotel company Accor was, for instance, a clear message about the accessibility of the firm to other cultures. Büring, who speaks fluent French and English and has extensive international management experience, was appointed in 1989 and made responsible for formulating the group's international human resource strategy. He was the first non-French manager to be given a place on the Accor board. He considers his appointment to have been a significant step in the company's internationalisation process: "Making me a member of the executive board has given the job of international human resources explicit importance throughout the group," he comments. "My position was created when the co-chairmen became sure that the real challenge of the 1990s was to create an efficient, motivated and qualified workforce worldwide."

Accor operates in 60 countries, but its business is still predominantly concentrated in its domestic market. Of the 779 hotels its owns, no less than 547 are based in France. Büring believes Accor needs to promote greater international mobility so as to create a more internationally thinking workforce. In particular, he is conscious that Accor's management cadres need to be more culturally diverse. Although indigenous managers head the group's various national subsidiaries, relatively small numbers of non-French managers occupy middle management positions or work at the group's corporate headquarters at Evry, on the outskirts of Paris. "We still need local people in our national organisations, but only by having more non-French at the corporate level will we be able to integrate the requirements of different national markets into our strategic reflections."

Clifford Chance also recognises the importance of internationalising its top management. It has been trying to bring in more non-British partners to the upper levels of its management team as it evolves from a UK organisation with subsidiary offices throughout the world to a flexible international network. The nearest equivalent to a senior management committee is the firm's "council". Until recently Clifford Chance was totally dominated by British lawyers, with only one representative from continental Europe. "We have taken steps to increase the number of European representatives," comments managing partner Geoffrey Howe, "so that the council better reflects, in purely numerical terms, the firm's geographical spread."

Management by travelling the globe

In the process of achieving an international climate, top managers act as powerful role models for the rest of the organisation. Electrolux, for example, holds the view that top managers need to be indefatigable travellers, taking the message to all parts of the globe. It believes that the vast amount of travelling done by the firm's senior and top managers is a vital part of the cement that binds Electrolux together. It encourages employees to see top management as normal regular visitors who want to discuss matters of common interest rather than "the bad guys from head office".

Electrolux's corporate centre has become a real presence throughout the organisation. If "management by wandering about" (MBWA) has become one of the slogans of the day, Electrolux's epithet might be more a matter of "management by travelling the globe" (MBTG). Kurt Vikersjö, Electrolux's executive development manager, stresses the importance of this aspect of the company's international spirit: "I think being an international manager implies that you must feel you are with friends wherever you are. If you dislike going to Italy, or don't like the USA, or feel that travelling around is just a necessary evil, then you are unlikely to succeed as an international manager in an organisation like Electrolux."

Senior executives who travel regularly at Grand Metropolitan, the UK-based international food, drinks and retailing business, see their role as helping managers in GrandMet's overseas businesses to "think globally and act locally". Frequent travellers, they have been dubbed "bag carriers". Their functions include: agreeing appropriate objectives with national managers and reviewing business proposals; protecting the integrity of brands so that their positioning remains consistent; ensuring national managers maintain high professional standards; and identifying and encouraging any best practice which is transferable across national and cultural boundaries. To develop an international outlook in its "bag carriers", GrandMet runs three-day "international awareness" classes which take managers to different countries to undertake practical work.

Signalling commitment to internationalisation

There are many other ways in which top management can signal allegiance to a firm's international activities. For example, some companies hold board meetings away from the parent country to show commitment to the firm's operations in a particular region. In June 1987, ICI's main board met in New York, the first time in the company's history that it had come together outside the UK. The meeting reflected the company's growing presence in the North American market. In June 1988, the ICI board held a meeting in Paris to show it's commitment to the creation of a single European market.

Multinational events such as conferences and seminars are one of the most common ways of building an organisation's culture and can serve as a platform for promoting core values. Many of the firms featured in this book hold regular get-togethers for people from different parts of the world to share interests, experiences and information. In 1990, for example, Accor ran a "summer university" at its training academy at Evry. This was a one-week management development programme for senior managers from all around the world. About 70 people attended and received training in all aspects of cultural awareness.

The Fiat conference system
The Italian car manufacturer Fiat explicitly views such occasions as a means of fostering greater unity in the company. Concerned to increase the international orientation of its managers and to expand their international awareness, it introduced a wide-ranging "internationalisation of management" project. One aspect of this initiative has been greater attention to international communications within the company. Fiat now organises conferences for the managers of its companies operating abroad. Managers from France, Spain, Portugal, Brazil and the USA have been able to meet with top managers from Fiat's head office and the Fiat sectors to learn more about the company and its workings. The conferences offer probably the first opportunity for many managers in these countries to meet people from other Fiat companies in the same country.

An integral part of Fiat's "internationalisation of management" project has been to revamp company in-house publications to create wider international perspectives among the company's managers and to give them more knowledge about the company's operations in different countries. The company's news bulletin for executives and managers, *In Diretta*, is now published monthly in five different languages. *Dossier International*, a new bilingual publication in Italian and English, also aimed at managers, appears every 4–6 months and provides a "lively survey of the most significant events affecting the group". *Fiat Quadri* and *Illustrato Fiat* aim to broaden the horizons of Fiat employees with a series of articles on the countries where companies in the group operate.

Like Fiat, other more enlightened international groups give careful attention to their in-house international communications. Unilever's in-house journal *Unilever Magazine* is a splendidly informative and lively publication which provides regular information about Unilever activities around the world. Other firms covered by the Ashridge survey pointed to the promotion of an "international outlook" not only through in-house magazines and newsletters but also through other media like annual reports, exhibitions, and induction videos, all of which can restate a company's management philosophy and reinforce its international identity.

Some firms also supplement communications by providing on-the-spot experience for employees. For instance, one Swedish company organises subsidised group visits to subsidiary companies overseas, while a Finnish firm arranges for trade-union leaders to make visits abroad to see the company's international operations for themselves. Educating union representatives about the value of overseas business is a wise step for the growing number of firms with international workforces outnumbering the people they employ in the original parent country.

IT and networking

Companies today have the means to move information about their organisations electronically at high speed. Networking, the ability to develop a web of co-operative relationships and informal alliances across the organisation, linked together by state-of-the-art technology, is becoming a valuable tool for spreading an international spirit.

As Chapter 1 showed, companies all over the world are waking up to the fact that their formal hierarchical structures are no longer capable of handling the plethora of knowledge and information generated by an ever more complex and fast-moving international environment. A key success factor will be the ability to promote organisational learning by the rapid transfer of knowledge and information between different parts of the organisation. More and more, this will depend on nurturing "networks of opportunity" that transcend country boundaries and formal reporting lines. What this means in practice is that when managers in any one subsidiary need to find expertise or information quickly they will know where to find it elsewhere in the organisation without referring back to head office. Much depends on the willingness, not to say eagerness, of managers in one part of the firm to share their experience with others – to move beyond "power hug".

The new challenges of the global business arena are summed up by Richard Giordano, chairman of the BOC Group. The most difficult task facing companies in the 1990s, he says, is organisational mastery of scale and complexity. Companies must master forms of organisation which reach beyond traditional concepts of delegation and profit centres. Such organisations will have to be internally flexible, interactive and interdependent, and will be required to do business at great distances across national boundaries and cultures.[4]

Many international firms recognise that a global telecommunications network greatly helps to knit together far-flung subsidiaries and forge a common approach. While significant advances in information technology, such as teleconferencing and electronic mail, are helping to achieve swifter and more intimate forms of communication, there are still problems to overcome. The subsidiaries of international companies, particularly those with a high degree of autonomy, tend to develop their own IT systems which are often incompatible with those of the parent company or those of other subsidiaries throughout the group. Each subsidiary is reluctant to change its system to fit with the rest and there can often be a resistance to making locally stored information available for general use. It can appear to the subsidiaries that their autonomy is under threat.

BOC and systems architecture

BOC appointed its first director of information technology in 1989 to come to grips with such issues and to develop a consistent and compatible systems architecture throughout the world. Neil Twist, the man entrusted with the job, was no IT expert. He had spent 20 years with BOC as a general manager. But the appointment of a generalist to co-ordinate BOC's worldwide IT policy was no accident. BOC's operating managers throughout the world are the ones who have the ultimate responsibility for applying IT to their businesses. BOC believed, therefore, that where persuasion was required, it would be best if it came from a generalist who could speak the managers' own language. Twist made a predictable discovery within a short while of taking up the new job: "What I found in the first few months was that we had lots of islands of IT around the world that didn't communicate very well with one another." Such IT islands develop from their own rationale, making sense within their own national context, and are often guarded jealously by their creators.

With this problem in mind, Twist has set himself a major goal – "to get good networking going between IT professionals within the group". But after surveying the diversity of IT equipment used by BOC companies around the world, Twist does not underestimate the task ahead of him:

> "It sometimes looks as though our individual business units all went to a vendors' convention and tried to be nice to everybody. We have hardware and software which is as varying as it can be. It's not surprising. It would be remarkable if it was anything else. The real disadvantages are only now becoming apparent and will begin to hurt more and more in the future unless we do something about them because we want more and more to become a global company."

One electronic tool that BOC increasingly uses is E-mail (electronic mail). E-mail systems allow users to send information rapidly to each other from desk to desk and increasingly from outside locations – from home, from offices in other countries and (with the use of portable modems) while travelling the world. BOC has initiated a project called GEMS – Group Electronic Mail Services – with the aim, as Twist puts it, of "connecting as many of these islands of office automation as possible, because I passionately believe that this is one of a series of tools which actually help to break down the barriers between human communications throughout the group".

But advances in IT, however ingenious, are only tools to achieve a wider goal. "It's actually a vision about how the company ought to be run and the value system it ought to have in the future."

Ericsson's networks

Ericsson, according to senior vice-president Britt Reigo, is "built on networks. Without these networks it would fall apart. The whole of

Ericsson is a system. We have different business areas but we are very dependent on each other." But while Ericsson's informal network is very effective, as might be expected of a company that is moving towards the development of total communications systems, it is difficult to enter it as a newcomer. In the past, most Ericsson managers working in key positions outside Sweden have been Swedes. It has therefore been a very Swedish network and many local employees have been excluded. The company is determined to change this state of affairs in future in order to hold on to good local people. Ericsson is striving to find ways to bring "outsiders" into its "global network" and the management education programmes it has been introducing are seen as an important instrument for achieving this.

Networking and decentralisation at Accor

Accor also declares its aim of rapidly becoming a networking organisation where resources and expertise can flow freely through different countries and business segments. This represents the second phase of a decentralisation policy which began in the early 1980s when the group organised itself into more focused business divisions, consisting of about 350 profit centres, to facilitate greater autonomy and accountability among its staff.

Achieving a networking organisation requires Accor's staff to adopt different mentalities and particularly to move beyond thinking in terms of national boundaries. In fact, for Accor a networking structure is closely akin to the concept of the "boundary-less" organisation. Both rely on face-to-face contact and the free movement of people and resources; and both gain much of their internal cohesion through a strong collective philosophy, values and culture.

One way of promoting networking at Accor is through international strategic review meetings. Volker Büring explains:

> "The corporate centre does not control strategy. We have a top–down and bottom–up approach in keeping with our commitment to decentralisation. When we formulate our strategy we automatically gain feedback from the group. We also give people the opportunity to exchange experience and reflect on strategy by bringing people together regularly at conferences and workshops."

The "informal matrix" at Pepsi-Cola

Pepsi-Cola International also values the benefits of networking. As part of its approach, it holds a large number of meetings for employees from different parts of the world. These are often organised on functional lines, bringing together financial or technical personnel once a year to debate corporate strategy. They can also take the form of a gathering of PCI's franchise bottlers from different parts of the world to share knowledge and information. The human resources director, John Fulkerson, describes this as creating "a network and a wonderful synergy that allows you to get a lot of things accomplished. It helps to develop understanding, tolerance and willingness to accept new ideas such that, when someone has a good marketing idea somewhere, people will say: 'Let's use that in this country.'"

The need to create this kind of cross-fertilisation is why Pepsi-Cola puts so much emphasis on the importance of promoting an "informal matrix" that "cuts across functions, geographies, people and disciplines". The matrix is focused on problem-solving. To quote John Fulkerson again: "If somebody has an issue that they are working with, they can go and talk to anybody in any function, in any country, at any level of the organisation and ask them to help solve that problem." He stresses, however, that people must have attained a level of personal maturity so that they understand that others are trying to solve a problem and are not acting "politically".

Language development policy

Firms like Unilever, Fiat and NEC emphasise the importance of learning foreign languages to facilitate a free flow of communication throughout global organisations. The more far-sighted companies realised early on in their progression towards multinational status that an inability to cope with a multiplicity of languages could be a serious impediment to smooth communications. Philips, the Dutch-based electronics giant, for example, rapidly concluded that the Dutch language, which is rarely used outside its own borders, could become a barrier to communications between its employees in different parts of the world and with its overseas customers. It took the decision at an early stage to make English the official company language. The company's international in-house magazine was published entirely in

English and it became rare for anyone in Philips to be promoted to any position of consequence unless an adequate mastery of English could be demonstrated.

This was no real handicap, however, to ambitious Philips' managers, since the Dutch have long displayed a remarkable facility for picking up foreign languages. Many of Philips' Dutch managers speak as a matter of course several European languages in addition to English. As a small country that had to look outwards to foreign markets in order to expand economically, the Netherlands has a long tradition of coming to grips with different cultures.

For quite a number of years, however, the universal language policy of Philips stopped short of the boardroom at its headquarters in Eindhoven. The company has always been fiercely proud of its local family origins and for many years resisted pressure to co-opt non-Dutchmen on to its supervisory and management boards. There was therefore no requirement to hold the board meetings in any language other than Dutch. The exclusivity was finally breached with the appointment of a Belgian to one of the company's top management groups. Ironically, there was still no reason for the Philips' board to converse in English because he was a native Flemish speaker.

While English is becoming the *lingua franca* of international business, this should be no cause for complacency for companies from the English-speaking world. It does not automatically provide an advantage for them in international markets. Non-British managers may be able to understand each other more easily when speaking English together than they can understand a native English-speaker. A German firm, for instance, is said to have awarded a contract to a Finnish company rather than a British firm because it believed that there would be fewer difficulties in speaking English with the Finns. While the Germans and the Finns were not totally fluent in English, communication between them was easier than with British managers who speak in a more articulate, but less comprehensible, manner.

Richard Giordano, chairman of BOC, believes that the spread of English around the world has hidden dangers for English-speaking countries. "The biggest challenge we face in exploiting the full potential of networking is cultural," he declares.

"The forging of an American management culture [as at BOC] was relatively easy compared to the task we now face in achieving the same result with our Far Eastern associates. Obviously, our transatlantic companies share many common traditions, and perhaps even a similar language. I am impressed with the rate at which our Chinese and Japanese managers and employees are learning English. I am very disappointed at the rate at which their British and American counterparts in our company are learning Chinese and Japanese. The proliferation of English around the world can create dangerous complacency. They may be speaking to us in English, but they are still thinking and feeling in their own language."[5]

Giordano's observations are borne out by NEC, Japan's giant electronics group, where corporate capability in English has become an indispensable factor in the company's ability to develop internationally and where the continual upgrading of English-language competence has strategic importance. The kind of integrated global networking that NEC has set out to create is simply not possible without thousands of its employees who work in technical and nontechnical functions having a reasonable competence in the English language.

The same is true of other major Japanese corporations. Yet its significance is rarely, if ever, grasped by foreign writers on Japanese business and management because in their countries foreign-language instruction is either an irrelevant issue (as is generally the case in the USA and Britain) or is merely seen as an unexceptional aspect of training. Of all the major industrial countries, only in Japan can foreign-language capability be considered an element of international corporate strategy.

NEC's International Education Division employs two Americans and one Scot for teaching English and cross-cultural communication, but other native speakers of English, hired on a freelance basis, are available at another training centre on the outskirts of Tokyo. Instruction in English is not just directed at oral proficiency for day-to-day business contact, but also seeks to improve skills in business presentation and "rhetoric" (that is how to handle arguments with foreigners, a notorious weakness of the Japanese). There are also several courses, especially for technical authors, on technical writing and editing in English.

NEC employees are encouraged to attend the various categories of English-language instruction, and any special prowess is likely to come to the notice of the company's department of human resource development. In this way, there is harmonisation between language learning and international business planning.

Language training at NEC is conducted in small groups and makes use of three types of media: instructional videos, topical items taken from the English-language press, and company-related case studies. Videos supplement cross-cultural training sessions with English the language of discussion. Press material is taken from English-language newspapers published in Japan as well as leading international publications like the *New York Times* and *Financial Times*. The selection of the articles normally aims to make participants more aware of how the rest of the world views Japan and in effect to learn in the classroom the art of countering "Japan bashing".

Company case studies, translated from Japanese into English, are a particularly interesting method of sensitising employees to the pitfalls of cross-cultural misunderstandings. NEC's personnel department encourages staff returning to Japan to write up some aspect of their experiences which might be illuminating for those who follow.

Sir Michael Angus, Unilever's UK chairman, believes that language skills are important not simply for communication but because "it is part of approaching customers and markets in a professional way. It is the key to operating effectively across cultural barriers. An ease with foreign languages is inevitably accompanied by growing familiarity with different places and cultures."[6]

Some companies believe that a commitment to language training sends a strong message to their employees that the organisation must be internationally, rather than nationally, oriented. If firms are to invest in language training, however, they must consider it as part of the firm's strategic plan, not as an isolated activity.

That most British firms and managers have far to go in language training is borne out by a survey by the British Institute of Management.[7] According to the results of this survey, fewer than half of British managers can understand a simple business letter in French.

The institute sent business letters in French, German, Spanish, and Italian to 3,000 managers. Of those responding to the survey, 44 per cent understood the French version, 14 per cent the German, 5 per cent the Spanish, and 5 per cent the Italian. The results were even worse when managers were asked whether they could reply to the letters in the same language. Only 23 per cent believed they could reply in French, 9 per cent in German, and 2 per cent in Spanish and Italian. The survey concluded that British managers have an unshakeable belief that English is the business language of the world and that other languages are unnecessary.

Internationalism is a long-term aim

The British are not alone in their insularity. But perhaps we should not dwell too much on the legacies of the past. The impact of a single European market and the globalisation of the world economy will force internationalism on even the most inward-looking companies.

Each company will take its own route towards achieving an international spirit, but there is plenty of evidence to suggest that those organisations that make a concerted effort to devise a formal and properly thought-out policy, as opposed to an ad hoc approach, are those most likely to make good progress. Companies that are moving in this direction recognise, however, that internationalism cannot be achieved overnight.

Fiat, for example, believes that the real pay-off from its internationalisation of management project will come in the longer term. Nevertheless the company believes the project has already led to a greater integration between its Italian and non-Italian managers and that its top management is now much more visible in the countries where Fiat operates. The way forward, it says, is "the consolidation of a company culture which is growing increasingly sensitive to its international context". What makes a company international are its "internal values, its actions and the way its activity is accepted and expressed, and not merely its location and how it operates".

Internationally minded companies see that the international spirit needs to permeate every facet of business life. Accor, for one, sees business strategy and human resource strategy as being inextricably linked.

"In order to realise business strategy, a certain type of organisational structure must be in place. The efficiency of such a structure is determined by the motivation and qualifications of people. What happens if these people are not suitably qualified? At best they might change your structures – at worst they might force you to change direction because you do not have the human resources with which to implement your strategy."

Accor is convinced that to become a truly global business it must have in place systems and resources that allow the development of all its employees worldwide.

★ ★ ★ ★

There are some people who will worry that an international spirit threatens to undermine or to dilute the unique qualities of local culture. Let the last word here go to Unilever with its long experience of working with many different cultures. Its chairman, Sir Michael Angus, says: "I don't believe that having a common company culture really means that you have to subjugate local attitudes and local cultures. A shared understanding of where the business is going, how it's going to get there and how we do things is not at all inconsistent with local pride."[8]

References

1. M. Silva and B. Sjögren, *Europe 1992 and the New World Power Game*, Wiley, New York, 1990.
2. G. Hofstede, *Culture's Consequences: International Differences in Work-Related Values*, Sage Publications, Beverley Hills & London, 1980.
3. T. Wilkinson, "TI's quest for a global culture", *The Independent*, August 21, 1990, p. 19.
4. R. Giordano, 1990 Stockton Lecture to London Business School, published in *BOC Management Magazine*, no. 20, May 1990, pp. 5-16.
5. R. Giordano, 1990 Stockton Lecture, *op. cit*.
6. "Challenges for Business Leaders in the 1990s". Speech by Sir Michael Angus to the MBA graduation ceremony, Ashridge Management College, May 11, 1990.
7. G. Pearce, *Bonjour Europe – Language and the British Manager*, British Institute of Management, Corby, 1991.
8. Cited in "Globesmanship", *Across the Board*, January/February 1990, pp. 24-34.

CHAPTER 4

WHAT IS AN INTERNATIONAL MANAGER?

The Ashridge survey and the subsequent research into the companies featured in this book confirm that a number of attributes are universally desirable in an international manager. We consider these in the first part of this chapter. It is also clear, however, that each firm needs to consider how its own strategy and structure affect its particular requirements. We accordingly look at how firms such as Ericsson, Fiat and Price Waterhouse Europe have determined the characteristics they want in their managers. When a company carries out this kind of exercise it is likely to find, like some of these firms, that there is more than one kind of international manager and that more people than previously suspected have a significant international dimension to their work.

THE KEY CHARACTERISTICS

So what are the basic qualities that all companies look for? As a starting-point in our investigations, the Ashridge survey asked companies to select the five most important characteristics required of the international managers in their organisation. Significantly, four of the six most important characteristics chosen by the surveyed companies are "soft" skills, as opposed to "hard" or functional skills, which were rated as a relatively low priority (see Table 4.1 on page 69). This underlines the sensitivity needed to manage people from other countries and unfamiliar situations.

Strategic awareness

The most important attribute required by international managers, according to the survey results, is strategic awareness. One company

Table 4.1 **Key characteristics of the international manager**
(% of respondents who ranked a characteristic as among the five most important)

	%
Strategic awareness	71
Adaptability in new situations	67
Sensitivity to different cultures	60
Ability to work in international teams	56
Language skills	46
Understanding international marketing	46
Relationship skills	40
International negotiation skills	38
Self-reliance	27
High task-orientation	19
Open, non-judgemental personality	19
Understanding international finance	13
Awareness of own cultural background	2

Source: The Ashridge survey, 1989–90.

described this as the necessity for managers to have a "global view of their own contribution", while another firm said that it wanted managers who did not think too narrowly but who could focus on issues outside their subsidiaries.

Strategic awareness is the competence most highly valued by Varity, the North American-based industrial management company, in its attempts to achieve international effectiveness. According to Alan Don, Varity's vice-president for organisation and executive planning, the key questions that companies should ask themselves are: "Where is the business going? Do we have sustainable competitive advantages in our business? If not, what are they and how do we get them?"

Strategic awareness calls for managers who can physically operate across different national boundaries as well as for individuals who travel mentally by understanding the international implications of their work. Companies need to develop both kinds of international mobility.

Johnson & Johnson has always been a company that values and

encourages entrepreneurship throughout its organisation. It recognises that people are not always willing to sublimate their own desires to the general benefit, and sees that it now needs to develop managers who are also "willing to look outside their own businesses and are willing to be team participants with other J&J managers". This becomes particularly important as J&J seeks to consolidate such functions as production in overseas markets where previously independent J&J companies each had their own manufacturing operations.

The US group also hopes that by encouraging teamwork, managers will become more aware of the issues involved in organisational flexibility. One possibility being considered is to educate human resource staff about the issues so that they can act as "consultants to companies". The aim is that they should work with managers at all levels to encourage greater awareness of the issues of structure and flexibility.

One difficulty faced by J&J is that it operates in three dissimilar business sectors: consumer, pharmaceutical and professional. "The problem at the senior level is how do we get people to see the totality of the business?" explains Win Holzman, J&J's vice-president for organisation planning and development. This is an even greater problem in the USA because "our employees grow up in very narrow disciplines." This contrasts with the experience of some of the people in J&J's international companies who have had wider managerial experience and is one reason for bringing more managers from other countries into the ranks of senior management.

In discussions with companies, other dimensions to the international manager emerged. First, despite the low priority accorded to functional skills in the survey, the bedrock on which other skills are founded must be *professional and technical expertise*. As Varity observes, there is no point trying to develop international skills if the basic business expertise is lacking. While the company also values personal qualities, such as the ability to be comfortable with complexity and to understand a number of variables at one time, it is the professional disciplines required to manage its business process that are of prime importance. It is no good talking about international management development if managers do not understand business cycles and budgets and the other basics of running a business.

A global outlook

Our research also revealed that strategic awareness must be underpinned by a global outlook. Rhône-Poulenc, for example, says that its employees must think "world" and not "France". Similarly, General Electric seeks a vital quality in its international managers that Dr James Baughman, GE's corporate management development manager, calls "global brains", the capacity to apprehend world trends as they affect the business, to understand competitors on a global scale, and to appreciate the world standard of competition that is required to be a winner. This requires people to abandon parochial attitudes, held by citizens of most countries, regardless of their degree of economic development. In GE's case, it is not just a matter of encouraging a more global outlook in Americans. It also means helping managers of other nationalities "to open their eyes to a wider and faster playing field". "You might have won your local city swimming championship and then you go on to the national championship. Then you get to the Olympics and you see the first 15 swimmers separated by a thousandth of a second and you realise that the global standard of play is quite a bit faster than at home."

Baughman believes that chief among the qualities that predispose a person to a global outlook is curiosity, followed by openness. "Some people sit on a plane and strike up a conversation with the person next to them; some people don't. Some people are curious about other parts of the world and some people aren't." He considers these qualities are largely innate, but that they can be enhanced through training, development and the sharing of "best practices".

Inter-cultural competence

The ability to think globally must be balanced with a sensitivity towards the individual's own national or local context, the often-cited maxim that international managers must "think globally and act locally". We prefer to describe this ability more specifically as inter-cultural competence. Although self-awareness of the manager's own cultural background received a low priority in the Ashridge survey, the evidence presented by researchers like Geert Hofstede (see Chapter 3) reveals that an understanding of how one's own cultural roots influence one's personal outlook and management style is central to working effectively with other cultures.

Perspectives on handling cultural differences vary from company to company nonetheless. For example, Pepsi-Cola International, as a producer of a global brand, says that it is important to concentrate on the similarities between people, not the differences. On the other hand, Scandinavian Airlines believes that to deliver service internationally, it is vital to understand the values and expectations that lie behind people's behaviour in different cultures. In contrast, Unilever suggests that the first step to understanding another culture is to learn the language. Whatever actions companies take to heighten their managers' ability to manage across borders, however, it is important to avoid creating stereotypes about other nationalities and cultures.

Even those firms that emphasise professional skills and business competence above all else do not disregard the need for sensitivity to different countries and cultures. Alan Don of Varity admits that the company has had some failures through giving overseas assignments to people who lacked these qualities and some of its managers have had to be brought back prematurely to home base. "On international transfer, if that sensitivity is not there, then you've got failure on your hands. Some people are just genuinely interested in people of different cultures and some are not." Don believes, however, that genuine sensitivity is fundamentally difficult to identify and that often people who are thought to be culturally sensitive turn out otherwise.

The most internationally minded: the Ratiu research
In research conducted in the late 1970s, Indrei Ratiu of Paris-based Intercultural Management Associates tried to track down the qualities that make some people more inter-culturally adaptable than others. He questioned 250 young executives from 35 different nationalities attending two of Europe's leading schools for international managers: INSEAD at Fontainebleau in France and the London Business School.[1] Most of those questioned had at least three years' overseas experience and their average age was 27. All spoke at least two languages and all planned to continue international careers.

Ratiu asked: "What key learning experiences do you associate with your becoming more internationally minded?" The question was put to groups of executives who were considered to be highly internationally oriented and other managers perceived to be less international in their outlook.

He found sharp distinctions in the attitudes of the two groups. The so-called "most international" executives tended to be subjective and relative in their assessments, and to see others' views in the same way. They saw both themselves and their impressions as changing. The second, "less international" group of managers, on the other hand, spoke of themselves and the world as though they were relatively stable phenomena on which objective data can be gathered. They implied that the world is made up of cultures rather like a jigsaw puzzle: the picture of the whole can be expected to emerge from the sum of its parts.

This was graphically illustrated by the contrasting way each of the test groups regarded cultural stereotypes. The "most international" executives used them "self-consciously and tentatively", according to Ratiu, "as if recognizing the stereotype as no more than a temporary hold on an elusive reality". The other managers, by contrast, used stereotypes "unselfconsciously and conclusively, suggesting that the stereotype is indeed a valid and stable categorization that is somehow inherent in the world 'out there'."

Another distinguishing feature that Ratiu found in the "most international" managers was the ease and readiness with which they could recall and discuss the stress symptoms indicative of culture shock. The other managers claimed either never to have experienced culture shock or else referred to it "only obliquely and with discomfort". Ratiu believes that this supports other research findings that point to culture shock as being a positive learning experience.

The most internationally oriented managers had "stability zones" to which they could temporarily withdraw. The examples included diaries, hobbies, meditation and religious practice. The ability to withdraw temporarily arguably assisted these managers' involvement with unfamiliar environments.

To make sense of new experience, the most internationally oriented managers seemed to be concerned with getting a hold on *what* was going on. Their concern was with descriptions and interpretation rather than explanation. "As a way of making sense of new experience, this approach is essentially forward-looking," maintained

Ratiu. The less internationally inclined managers, however, were more concerned with *why* things occur the way they do. Their emphasis was less on data collection and more on early explanation and rapid conclusions. In Ratiu's opinion, their approach was "essentially backward-looking".

These research findings led Ratiu to formulate an objective "macro-strategy" (red loop) which contrasts with a subjective "micro-strategy" (blue loop) for learning in cross-cultural situations (see Figure 4.1). But Ratiu stresses that there is more complexity to the inter-cultural learning process than this simplified model suggests.

Ratiu's research suggests that the managers most likely to succeed in an international environment are those who are flexible enough to be able to constantly reframe their fields of reference. Those who seek certainty, completeness, tidiness and rationality in everything they undertake are much less likely to accommodate to international mobility than those who can live in a less well-defined situation.

Managers who lack sensitivity to other cultures may suffer from ethnocentricity, says Robert T. Moran, professor of international

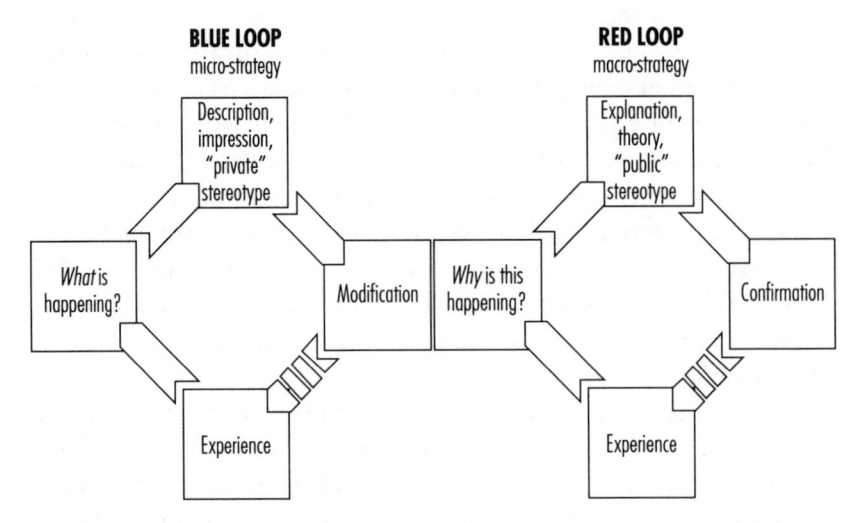

Figure 4.1 **International learning cycles: Blue loop v. red loop**

BLUE LOOP
micro-strategy

RED LOOP
macro-strategy

- Description, impression, "private" stereotype
- What is happening?
- Modification
- Why is this happening?
- Explanation, theory, "public" stereotype
- Confirmation
- Experience
- Experience

Reproduced from "Thinking Internationally", by Indrei Ratui, *International Studies of Management and Organization*, vol. XIII, no. 1–2, 1983, p.147, M. E. Sharpe, Inc.

studies and director of the programme of cross-cultural communications at the American Graduate School of International Management, Arizona. Moran defines "ethnocentrism" as "belief in the inherent superiority of one's own group and culture; it may be accompanied by feelings of contempt for those who do not belong; it views and measures alien cultures and groups in terms of one's own culture."[2] He insists it is something the international manager should strive to avoid. "How can one successfully communicate if he judges another culture's customs as foolish, ridiculous, or not quite as good as his own? Skilful international managers have learned to see the world differently and understand the way others manage and do business. This implies that there is no single way to do anything."

Moran singles out empathy as an important quality that helps international managers to adjust to new cultures and to succeed in their jobs. He explains: "The Japanese word *omoiyari* expresses the idea of empathy well. It means understanding, but it also implies a communication, often non-verbal, of rapport and acceptance." Ethnocentrism and empathy are of course opposites. "If one believes in the superiority of one's group and culture and has feelings of contempt towards others, it is impossible to walk in their shoes."

Women as international managers

International management has traditionally been a masculine preserve. Many of the firms that Ashridge talked to, however, were aware of the need to do much more to open up international career paths for women.

According to an article in *International Management*,[3] a magazine that circulates to top executives around the world (97 per cent of them male), women in France and the USA represent an estimated 40 per cent of MBA graduates and in Belgium about 36 per cent. Women launch 40 per cent of all new businesses in western Germany and 42 per cent in Britain. A study by Nancy J. Adler from McGill University, Montreal, nevertheless revealed that of 13,338 expatriates from American and Canadian companies, only 3 per cent were women.[4] This is the more surprising in that further investigation by the same researcher[5] indicated that women possess social skills that make them particularly suitable for international management. She questioned 52 female expatriate managers while on assignment in Asia or after returning from Asia to North America. The reported disadvantages of being female had more to do with the attitudes of their own companies than with the international assignments themselves.

The women reported numerous professional assets from being female. Most frequently, they described the advantage of being highly visible. Foreign clients were curious about them, wanted to meet them, and remembered them after the first meeting. It was therefore somewhat easier for the women than for their male colleagues to gain access to foreign clients' time and attention.

The women also described the advantages of good interpersonal skills and their observation that men could talk more easily about a wider range of topics with women than with other men. This ease of interchange was especially important in cross-cultural situations, where difficulties of nuance and opportunities of miscommunication abound. "The women's ease was unforced and quite sincere, since it springs from fundamental socialization patterns," observed Adler.

> "I often take advantage of being a woman. I'm more supportive than my male colleagues ... Clients relax and talk more. And 50 per cent of my effectiveness is based on volunteered information." (woman expatriate working in Indonesia)

Many of the women expatriates whom Adler questioned spoke of a higher status accorded them in Asia. Despite the low social status extended to indigenous women in that part of the world, the expatriates felt they received special treatment not given to their male colleagues. Most of the women claimed benefits from a "halo effect". Since their foreign colleagues and clients had seldom or never worked with a female expatriate manager, they knew it was highly unusual for North American firms to send female managers to Asia. Thus the Asians tended to assume that the women would not have been sent unless they were the best. Therefore they expected them to be "very, very good".

The problems the women did experience were most often with their home companies rather than their Asian clients. For instance, after obtaining a foreign assignment, some women found that their company imposed limits to their opportunities and job scope while they were abroad. More than half the female expatriates described difficulties in persuading their home companies to give them the same latitude as given to their male colleagues, especially initially. Some companies, out of concern for the women's safety, limited their travel and excluded them from postings to remote, rural and underdeveloped areas.

Nancy Adler concluded that female expatriates often enjoy significant pluses in a highly competitive atmosphere. She suggested that their successes abroad draw on "characteristics that have traditionally been a fundamental part of the female role in many cultures – their great sensitivity, communication skills, and ability to establish rapport. Women need not buy into the competitive game. They can subtly shift the interaction out of the power and dominance modes so typical of business interchange – and so highly dysfunctional in cross-cultural relations – into the sort of co-operative, collaborative modes becoming increasingly important today."

These research findings are endorsed by a small survey of international women managers by Ashridge, carried out in 1990. The participants, working in a wide range of countries, also underlined the special qualities that make women effective as international executives. A Swiss executive who has worked in six different countries and runs her own consultancy and training business, referred to women's "increased sensitivity for people's concerns". She also suggested that "being members of a minority culture" gives women a better understanding of other cultures.

A British manager specialising in electronic banking, who has worked in Hong Kong and Malaysia, observed that women's higher level of interpersonal sensitivity was especially important when managing multi-cultural people or projects. Being able to understand – or even just recognise – that differences in attitudes or views may be deep rooted within a culture, gives a better opportunity to work around potential problems. "Similarly, I feel women are more flexible in their approach to problem-solving and aim to achieve results by the most suitable method rather than the 'standard' method."

Other female attributes brought to light by the Ashridge survey included the suggestion that women are better at learning foreign languages; have "stronger teaching/coaching skills and are more flexible in negotiating"; have good market knowledge because they are buyers and consumers; and are accustomed, by their traditional social roles, to working under pressure and dealing with many things at the same time. A German respondent added that they were good team workers and less bossy.

There is a growing body of research to suggest that women are particularly effective at networking. Studies show that women's behaviour patterns emphasise precisely those values and attitudes which are important for networking, such as sensitivity, communication, community, sharing and relationships. Women seem to be more concerned about the social dimension of work and more inclined to view work relationships as friendships. They are also more inclined than men to listen and pay attention to other points of view.

Since many of these attributes are qualities sought after in the international manager, firms would do well to consider how they can provide better opportunities for women to take a more equal role internationally. Very few of the women managers interviewed for the Ashridge survey could however name any specific steps that their companies were taking to help women take up more international roles.

THE INTERNATIONAL MANAGER AS LEADER

Several of the qualities that companies listed as high priorities fall under the general category of leadership. Its importance is summed up by GE's James Baughman: "You can be a business virtuoso and very much a person of the world, but unless you also have leadership, you will not be equal to the demands of being a world player. You have to have that something which makes people want to follow you. We have to have people who excel at team play and excel at leading team play."

What constitutes leadership ability? According to Unilever, managers need to be high-achievers with strong ego needs. On the other hand, in working across borders, they also need to have "humility" and strong affiliation instincts. People who are capable of combining these characteristics are relatively rare and Unilever recognises that it will be no easy task expanding their numbers. Tony Vineall, the company's deputy director of personnel, responsible for worldwide management development, cites approvingly the American chief executive who said that he wanted to recruit "eagles who are happy to fly in formation".

The Ericsson model

Ericsson's leadership model similarly acknowledges that the international leadership qualities that it has identified, such as self-esteem and respect for others, do not always co-exist in the same person. As part of its general strategy to make a more concerted effort to tap its international talent, the Swedish company assigned a taskforce to draw up a profile of the effective Ericsson manager. What emerged was a leadership model which envisaged "human" and "task" skills (interpersonal skills and professional/technical ability) building on a base of "individual capacities" (see Figure 4.2 on page 80).

Individual capacities include the following:

- *Intellectual ability*. Ericsson produces complex and technologically advanced products. This means that it is vital for managers to have a quick and agile intellect characterised by the ability to identify problems, see openings and connections, and collect and select relevant information. In addition they need the ability to analyse a situation in a creative and rational way and to find feasible solutions.
- *Self-esteem*. Managers must have a realistic and thorough degree of self-knowledge, self-confidence and self-acceptance. He or she should be stable and secure and know what they want. This basic stability allows the individual to be open and flexible.
- *People-orientation*. The person must show a genuine interest in and respect for others and have a basic trust in people. They must have the ability to communicate with others and the will and ability to work with others. Such people stimulate an open working atmosphere, are fair and just towards others and make unprejudiced decisions. Ericsson recognises that

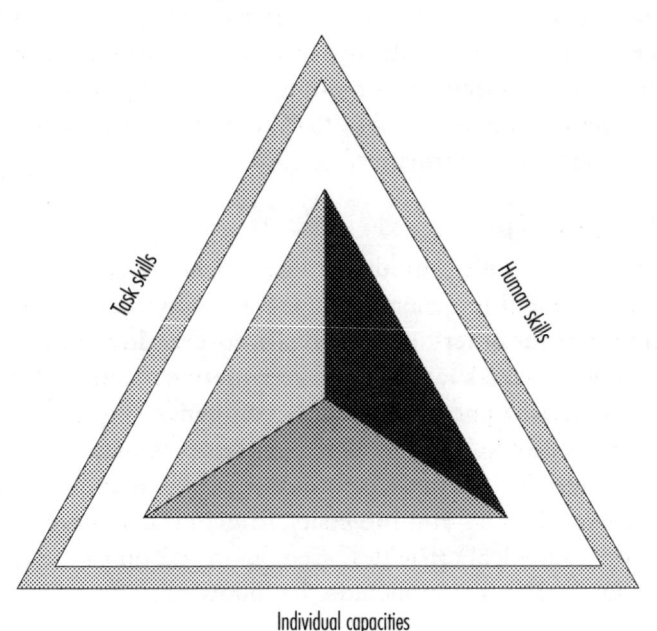

Figure 4.2 **The Ericsson leadership model**

Task skills
Human skills
Individual capacities

Source: Ericsson

these attributes are not always well-developed in technical organisations.
- *Perspective*. This is the ability to comprehend the whole situation yet focus on what is essential. It entails the ability to shift perspective, to see both the entirety and the details. It also means that the person can accommodate both the company's and the unit's interests.
- *Results-orientation*. This boils down to the will and the ability to initiate tasks and obtain results. It demands initiative and perseverance and involves the ability to make decisions, act and take responsibility even in situations that are marked by risk and uncertainty. It also means the ability to set high, but realistic, goals.

Ericsson believes that to some degree these attributes are inherent in people. "It is not possible to develop these characteristics from zero.

You have to have a base from which to start." The company now uses this model to evaluate first-time managerial candidates and the potential of managers for other positions. It also hopes that the leadership model will help to create a common language that any of its people anywhere in the world can use when selecting managers.

TEAM MEMBERSHIP

If the future can be expected to put a premium on leadership ability, it will also call for team membership skills. The companies in the survey ranked these highly, realising the extra skills involved in working in multi-disciplinary and multi-cultural teams. The complexity of prevailing conditions will in future demand joint approaches to problem-solving and a collegial style of leadership. The team leader will frequently have to defer to the experience and expertise of other team members. In recognition of this, one objective of General Electric's action learning projects is to give senior managers who are used to being the boss in their own businesses experience of working in teams and co-operating with others.

Like Johnson & Johnson, Pepsi-Cola International has always cherished entrepreneurship. It believes, however, that independence and initiative should be balanced by teamwork. Dr John Fulkerson, the company's director of human resources, says: "If you've got a problem, it's OK to ask for help. Like the notion of instant feedback, asking for help can be a good thing." Providing help is very much the role of Pepsi-Cola's corporate centre. "We use the phones a lot, travel a lot, get out there working with the people, and use communication to overcome traditional barriers of time and distance."

The international manager will increasingly find him or herself working in multinational teams. While culturally diverse teams have high potential for creativity, the differences in values and behaviour of team members from different cultural backgrounds may pose obstacles to effective teamworking.

Cultural variations and team attitudes

J. Malcolm Rigby, a US consultant who works with multinational teams, has found that two of the dimensions of cultural variation identified by Geert Hofstede (see Chapter 3), "power distance" (how people view and relate to authority) and "uncertainty avoidance" (how people feel about ambiguous situations), are the most likely to cause problems in such teams.[6] In cultures with "high" power distance, such as the Philippines and Mexico, people typically accept that power in organisations is distributed unequally and take a positive view of directive, paternal and autocratic management styles and methods of decision-making. They will be more fearful of openly disagreeing with the boss than would members of "low" power distance cultures such as the USA, the UK or Australia. They will have difficulty in situations requiring openness, frankness and feedback. Members from "low" power distance backgrounds, on the other hand, may at times be too open and confrontive.

Similarly, managers from "high" uncertainty avoidance cultures, such as Japan and Greece, tend to be highly concerned with security, need structure and respect, require rules and regulations, and prefer clear-cut and detailed instructions. They also have a strong need for consensus and consider conflict and competition within the group as undesirable. They strongly fear failure and may be less prepared to take risks than people from "low" uncertainty avoidance cultures, such as Americans, Swedes, or the British.

It is all too easy for British or American team members, who come from "low" power distance and "low" uncertainty avoidance countries and who may tend to believe in the efficacy of "straight talk" in solving problems, to become bored and disenchanted with their colleagues from "high" power distance and "high" uncertainty avoidance countries, such as Japan, Greece or France; and vice versa. It is hardly surprising, therefore, that although multi-cultural teams with their rich multiplicity of perspectives have the potential to be the most effective and productive teams, they very often turn out to be the least productive.

In a very useful book that summarises the findings of various researchers who have investigated the international dimensions of organisational behaviour, Nancy Adler of McGill cites research into multi-cultural teams at the University of California (UCLA).[7] This suggests that culturally diverse teams tend to be either the most or the least effective, while the performance of homogeneous teams tends to be average. The critical factors are the nature of the task facing the team, the team's stage of development and the way in which diversity is managed.

UCLA found, for example, that multi-cultural teams work better on tasks requiring innovation than on routine tasks where it is helpful if all members think and behave similarly. Also, diversity is generally most valuable during the planning and development of projects, when it enables the team to benefit from new perspectives and ideas and to formulate alternative approaches. It may be less helpful in the earlier stages when the team needs to develop cohesiveness. It becomes a problem again later, during the implementation stage, when the team needs to agree, or converge, on which decisions and actions to take.

What can the manager do to maximise the creative benefits of cultural diversity and to minimise the disadvantages? Adler suggests that, where team leaders are able to select team members, they should pick people not only for their cultural background but also for their task-related abilities. Rather than ignoring or downplaying cultural differences, team members should recognise the differences by describing the range of cultures present without attempting to interpret or evaluate them.

Mutual respect among team members is vital and managers can enhance it by by making members' prior accomplishments and task-related skills known to the group. Because culturally diverse groups have more trouble than homogeneous teams in agreeing on what constitutes a good or bad idea or decision, it is important to give teams early positive feedback on their performance, both as individuals and groups. In particular, feedback from an external source, such as a manager from outside the group, can help the group to see itself as a team and can teach it to value its diversity, recognise the contributions of individuals, and to trust its collective judgement.

One of the most important things that the manager can do is to help the group to agree on a superordinate goal that transcends individual differences. This can provide direction and focus for the team and will be reinforced by the company's wider efforts to foster an international spirit. The manager may indeed actually relate the team's superordinate goal directly to the core values and objectives espoused by the firm. It is then, in a sense, the firm's international spirit writ small.

NETWORKING SKILLS

To be fully effective in the international learning organisations of the future, however, the international manager will have to look beyond the immediate team. He or she will need to be able to exploit information, expertise and other resources wherever they might be found in the organisation worldwide. The ability to do this will depend in great measure on networking skills, an aptitude for developing a network of co-operative relationships and informal alliances across an organisation. This in turn depends on the willingness of the manager to acknowledge interdependence and to reciprocate favours. While there is a lot that can be done at a corporate level to encourage the formation of networks, it is up to managers themselves to go out and forge links and do it right from the start of their careers.

Managing relationships outside the formal chain of command calls for some special characteristics and interpersonal skills. These include initiative; willingness to share leadership; the ability both to talk and listen in conversations; willingness to take risks in expressing ideas and sharing information; the need to understand and accept differences. Networking, as Pepsi-Cola International verifies, also calls for a personal maturity that understands that others are not acting "politically". And networking across borders requires that individuals should have an awareness of how their own cultural roots might affect the way that they interact with others.

The networking skills the BOC Group seeks in its worldwide workforce have been outlined by Dick Giordano, its American-born chairman.[8] According to him, the BOC Group expects managers and technologists in its group companies throughout the world to take on their shoulders the responsibility for accessing group technology wherever it resides, and to keep appraised of, and implement, best practices in every aspect of their business.

Giordano explains the function of head office: "Our job at the centre is to facilitate communication and occasionally to audit. We keep a road map at the centre; a written and up-to-date technical inventory, telling us where the technology is and how it works rather than complete specifications for implementation." The centre issues publications, sponsors seminars and creates temporary committees to draw managers' attention to what is available and what is changing. It appoints "lead houses" for specific areas of technology or operational problems. A lead house may be in Sydney or Osaka, but will be identified as the most knowledgeable within the group on that subject. "It would have special responsibilities for dissemination of that knowledge to other group members around the world. We don't expect the work to be duplicated by other group companies." Overall, the small number of staff at the centre in Britain act on occasion as a "traffic policeman, sometimes as an orchestra conductor, and very often as a cheer-leader".

Giordano does not underestimate the effort that is necessary to build up and sustain a networking organisation, one that he defines as valuing speed and flexibility and which, above all else, recognises that delay is costly and sometimes fatal. He points out that such an organisation requires that managers live with more than average ambiguity and sometimes conflicting objectives.

> "In a sense, we are asking managers to be schizophrenic. In dealing with competitors outside the walls of the group, we employ all the metaphors of war and sport: win and lose, cut and thrust, go for the jugular and others even more colourful. Within the company we expect them to change garments and co-operate in a benign fashion. Not all managers are this flexible."

BOC has also come to recognise the important role that non-managerial staff play in a networking organisation. Often the links in the network are sustained by technical and functional personnel. This means that their quality and experience are increasingly important to the success of the business, giving BOC the challenge of fashioning rewards that reinforce their importance and allow them to develop careers outside the conventional corporate pyramid.

Currencies and exchange rates

Successful networking requires bypassing formal hierarchy structures and forging informal relationships. According to US management experts, David Bradford of Stanford University and Allan Cohen of Babson College, Massachusetts, the fundamental way to acquire influence without formal authority is through the "law of reciprocity" – "the almost universal belief that people should be paid back for what they do, that one good (or bad) deed deserves another".[9]

Bradford and Cohen suggest that people should use the metaphor of "currencies" and "exchange rates". In addition to organisation and technical knowledge, possible "currencies" that people can trade include "inspiration-related" currencies such as vision – being involved in a task that has a larger significance for the unit, company, customers or society; or a "position-related" currency such as involvement in a task that can aid promotion or advancement; or a "relationship-related" currency such as giving personal support.

The critical factor, the researchers point out, is to understand what is important to the person whom a manager wishes to influence – in effect, to understand what their exchange rate is. Managers must think about the other person as a potential ally, not an adversary. They need to know the other person's world, including their needs and goals. They need to be aware of key goals and available resources that the other person may value. And, they must seek mutual gain rather than "winner takes all".

The greater the extent to which the manager has worked with the potential ally and created trust, the easier the exchange process will be. Each knows the other's desired currencies and pressures and each will have developed a mutually productive interaction style. Less time is spent on figuring out the intentions of the ally, and there is less suspicion about when and where the payback will occur. Two issues are important: success in achieving task goals and success in improving the relationship so that the next interaction will be even more effective. Too often, say Bradford and Cohen, people who want to be effective concentrate on the task and act as if there is no tomorrow.

The international organisation is a storehouse of ideas and information representing different kinds of interest, experiences and perspectives. Without international networks and informal communication channels, those ideas and that information will remain locked in their boxes.

THE LIFE-LONG LEARNER

A rapidly changing international business arena will also require people to be life-long learners, as companies like Pepsi-Cola International realise. Most people who reach senior positions in Pepsi-Cola have had significant international experience. They have had to carry out a wide variety of tasks as the company does not maintain a large number of support staff. The challenges of their job demand a high degree of flexibility – the ability to formulate new courses of action when necessary – particularly in Pepsi-Cola's fast-moving international markets. For example, John Fulkerson cites the case of Mexico City where traffic congestion makes movement of products by big trucks impossible during the day and calls for some astute lateral thinking. "How do I fix it? ... Well, why not try night deliveries? Why not stack the product in little mini-warehouses so that during the day the salesmen can come along with his key and move the product with a hand truck? Now, that's distribution and that's the kind of flexibility that we're looking for."

This flexibility depends on an action-orientation, but one that is informed by creative thinking. "We want managers who think outside the box. We thrive on independence, personal initiative, a limited number of meetings, memos and formal communication. We much prefer to act."

General Electric similarly warns that "method actors" who go by the rule book will not succeed in international business. Robert Horton, chairman of BP, underscored this view when he said that "the successful international businessman is not automatically knowledgeable, but must learn very quickly. He finds experts on the countries he wants, and he has made himself a global expert on the industry in which he deals". In other words, the international manager must know how to learn.

THE FIAT EXPERIENCE

This chapter has identified some of the central competences demanded of international managers everywhere. There is more than one kind of international manager, however.

Different jobs have different types of international exposure. Fiat has identified four types of management post ranging from "transnational" to "local" positions. These came to light as a result of a survey of 30 key "opinion leaders" within Fiat and in leading European and US companies, carried out as part of the firm's "internationalisation of management" project. According to this survey, the ideal profile of the international manager at Fiat had the following characteristics (in order of priority):

- *Quality of know-how.* Interestingly this is seen to comprise not only professional expertise but also "inter-cultural competence", endorsing the research findings of Indrei Ratiu. For example, Fiat stresses the importance of inter-cultural awareness or "a particular sensitivity to the correct understanding and interpretation of other cultures". It also means, in Fiat's view, the ability to identify the values that influence managerial behaviour and company approaches in different cultural settings.
- *A strong identity.* This involves the ability to reconcile the necessary flexibility and openness that are needed for an affective exchange with other cultures with a firm grounding in the home culture.
- *Winning leadership.* This comprises both a results-orientation and the possession of a "charisma" that stems from "the highest level of professionalism".

In a follow up to this research, involving five project groups, Fiat discovered that international posts do not only involve expatriates. It became apparent that all jobs, wherever they are, have to contend with a "pluralistic context", that is to say they involve managing social, political, cultural, linguistic and technical differences. As Vittorio Tesio, Fiat's vice-president for management development and planning, puts it: "We discovered a simple truth. At the beginning of the research we thought that our international managers were the people we sent abroad. But we found that the real problem of the international manager is not linked to the people sent abroad. It is the people at home who have to manage the international structure."

This discovery helped Fiat to identify the four types of position that are exposed to internationalism to a greater or lesser degree. These are:

- *Transnational positions*: operating over the whole geographic area covered by a business.
- *Multinational positions*: operating in the context of several different countries.
- *Open, local positions*: operating within the context of a single country, with significant links, reference points and dependence on elements outside the country (generally head office).
- *Local positions*: operating within a single country, influenced by locally determined variables, without significant interaction with other countries.

This classification was used as the basis of a survey in 1988 to obtain a more detailed picture of Fiat's international dimension, which produced three significant findings. More than 40 per cent of the managerial jobs in Fiat deal with international matters. The most internationally exposed areas are the commercial, administrative, planning and – not least – the organisation and personnel sections. Three-quarters of the international positions in Fiat are to be found in Europe.

One of the Fiat project groups looked more closely at the qualities required of managers who work within the international framework:

1. Professional competence. This includes experience of running complex organisational units, specialist knowledge needed for the job and linguistic skills.

2. Managerial abilities. These concern the "operational" qualities that are critical for internationalisation:
- *Organisational*: the ability to plan and manage resources in order to fulfil a programme.
- *Problem-solving*: the capacity to analyse and resolve problems arising from new and unexpected challenges occurring outside the normal pattern of events.
- *Decision-making*: promptness and speed in making decisions and clarity in assuming or delegating responsibility.

- *Communications*: the ability to relate to people, to communicate clearly and to provide support in critical situations.
- *Leadership*: the ability to provide clear and decisive leadership in exercising authority.

3. Personal qualities. The individual skills needed in an international context are: openness to change; management of stress; and personal efficiency. In particular they include the ability to pick up signs of change and to keep moving in a situation characterised by uncertainty, and the will and determination to reach set targets.

4. Inter-cultural competence. Fiat has its own slant on what it means to work with other cultures. It involves, on the one hand, "a corporate self-identity", that is the ability to recognise and correctly interpret the values of the company culture. On the other hand, it is the ability to hold a dialogue with other cultures, that is to communicate and to represent the company's image abroad. Inter-cultural competence also involves being able to

Figure 4.3 **Fiat: Inter-cultural competence**

COMPANY IDENTITY

- 1 Promote the values of own culture
- 2 Understand other cultures
- 1 Communicate with other cultures
- 1 Negotiate successfully
- 2 Represent the company
- 2 Acquire valid experience

ABILITY TO CONDUCT A DIALOGUE WITH OTHER CULTURES

ABILITY TO INTERACT WITH OTHER CULTURES

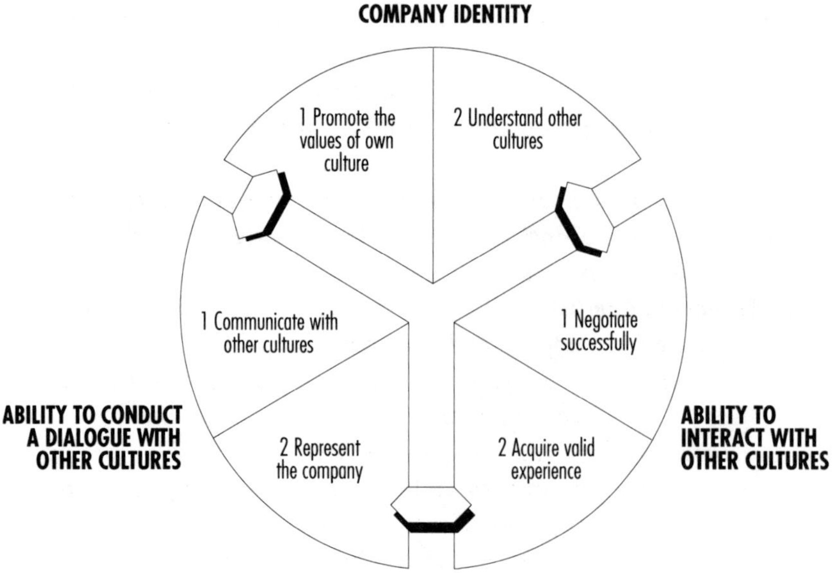

Source: Fiat

interact with other cultures including, very importantly, the ability to negotiate successfully, and the ability to build up and make the most of professional relationships with other cultures (see Figure 4.3 on page 90).

Fiat's Tesio emphasises the importance of maintaining the integrity of the company's cultural identity while being able to deal effectively with others:

"We don't need to imitate an external model, an American or British model. We are an Italian company with its own culture, not only an Italian culture but a strong company culture. We want people who are able to understand different cultures, who are able to communicate and exchange with cultures that are different from ours, and, what is more important, who are able to negotiate successfully with those cultures."

THE PRICE WATERHOUSE STUDY

Research carried out by Price Waterhouse Europe (PWE), the leading accounting and management consultancy group, into its own organisation revealed not only that the company has more than one different type of international manager, but also that there are many people in non-management jobs who also need an international perspective and skills. The latter is a fact so obvious that it is missed by many companies. Professional partnerships may well be more prone to this oversight because of their traditional emphasis on professional qualifications. They have a tendency to distinguish rigidly between two sets of staff known as "professional" and "support" staff or those who are "fee-earning" and "non-fee-earning".

Although support staff play a critical part in the success or failure of professional organisations and the way they are perceived by clients or potential clients, their role is often undervalued or insufficiently recognised. But as Naomi Stanford, the personnel manager responsible for training Price Waterhouse's support staff in Europe, points out, as firms extend their international, multinational and transnational base, high-calibre, valued support becomes even more essential. "Often support staff are the first contact that a potential client has with a firm. The skill with which the staff member handles another language or cultural differences and displays confident knowledge of the organisation, creates a lasting impression."

In order to understand more about the training needs of support staff, Stanford researched the nature of international management in the firm. She started by investigating the different types of international management that PWE managers are involved in by interviewing 12 managers with international responsibilities.

From this research emerged three distinct types of international manager – managers managing across boundaries from their native country; managers based abroad; and managers managing in their own country but needing to stay abreast of international trends, developments or ideas in other countries. It was apparent to PWE, therefore, that being an expatriate and managing projects in another country is only one of the ways in which a manager can regard him or herself as international. In fact, with the inclusion of the third category, almost all the managers in Price Waterhouse can be considered international. The international mind-set, therefore, is required of all levels and activities in the company.

PWE's research also established the following competences as crucial for international managers:

- ability to think strategically;
- analytical ability;
- knowledge of competitive markets, including knowledge of a specific country;
- knowledge of technological dynamics;
- ability to adopt perspectives other than their own;
- ability to work in both strategic and operating modes;
- ability to develop communication networks;
- knowledge of Price Waterhouse as a whole.

In addition to these central competences, language skills, political sensitivity, vision, creativity, imagination, realism, and the ability to propose and implement change were highly rated. Mobility and flexibility were also seen as significant.

The managers who were interviewed frequently emphasised the importance of an ability to develop communication networks and to communicate effectively. Everybody saw good communication as essential to business success: one manager indeed described his role as being "50 per cent orchestrating communication". Some of these qualities, though useful in any area of management, were said to assume special significance in an international context. This is particularly true of communication. In the international arena, ambiguity of communication can lead to serious misunderstandings. More than ever it is not enough to assume that because something has been communicated it has been understood.

In addition to the 12 managers, all but one of whom were partners in the firm, 14 secretarial and personal assistants were interviewed. Most of them had worked with their manager for less than two years. Both the secretary and the manager were asked to rank a list of skills on a continuum from "essential" to "not needed" in the support role.

High in the ranking came the need to have a knowledge of Price Waterhouse as a whole. Although secretaries were not required to be mobile and few travelled outside their own country as part of the job, the ability to make complex travel arrangements was seen as very important as were a knowledge of geography and location. Knowing where to obtain information was also regarded as vital.

The Price Waterhouse profile of international management competences identified the ability to develop communication networks with other people as an important attribute. Significantly, establishing and developing such networks was also one of the competences rated highly for support staff. They thus contribute to the success of their managers in one of the most important tasks in international management.

Secretaries and personal assistants need to be able to demonstrate initiative and flexibility; an ability to work closely with the manager at times, and at others to work without much supervision; for example, when managers are out of the country the secretary must act as their "anchor" and must know what needs to be passed on to them – and, perhaps more importantly, what is of low priority and can be left until they return.

★ ★ ★ ★

The characteristics of the international manager described in this chapter cannot be developed overnight. Most companies agree that managers' personal abilities to forge relationships and links with others, while partly innate and hence depending on selection, can be enlarged by training and experience. But this process depends in turn on the creation of an international spirit within the company as a whole.

Some management development specialists caution that even the largest international firms need to keep a sense of perspective when introducing policies to generate more globally aware executives. John Donegan, British Petroleum's group management development and training manager, warns that it is important to realise that "the demands of a global economy do not impact equally on all companies or on all managers within those companies. We must not assume that in the future even large multinationals will need to produce solely 'global' managers." In other words, an integrated management development strategy is called for, "based on a model of the impact of globalisation on the different structures and levels of the organisation".[10]

The following chapter examines two crucial issues. How can a company's international human resource strategy ensure that its managers acquire the appropriate attributes? And how can it do so in a way that reinforces the organisation's international spirit and builds its collective competence?

References

1 I. Ratiu, "Thinking internationally: A comparison of how international executives learn", *International Studies of Management and Organization*, vol. 13, no. 1-2, 1983, pp. 139-150.
2 R.T. Moran, series of articles for the "Cross-cultural contact" column of *International Management*, 1985-88.
3 L. Bernier, "Fear of flying", *International Management*, July/August 1988, pp. 55-59.
4 N.J. Adler, "Women in international management: Where are they?", *California Management Review*, vol. XXVI, no. 4, 1984, pp. 78-89.
5 N.J. Adler and M. Jelinek, "Women: World-class managers for global competition", *The Academy of Management Executives*, vol. II, no. 1, pp. 11-19.

6 J. Malcolm Rigby, "The challenge of multinational team development", *The Journal of Management Development,* vol. 6, no. 3, 1987, pp. 65-72.
7 Research by Dr Carol Kovach at the Graduate School of Management, University of California at Los Angeles. Cited in N.J. Adler, *International Dimensions of Organizational Behaviour,* Kent Publishing Company, Boston, Mass., 1986.
8 R. Giordano, 1990 Stockton Lecture at London Business School, published in *BOC Management Magazine,* no. 20, May 1990, pp. 5-16.
9 D.L. Bradford and A.R. Cohen, "Influence without authority: The use of alliances, reciprocity and exchange to accomplish work", *Organizational Dynamics,* Winter 1989, pp. 5-17.
10 J. Donegan, "The learning organisation: Lessons from British Petroleum", *European Management Journal,* vol. 8, no. 3, September 1990.

CHAPTER 5

MAKING MANAGERS INTERNATIONAL

Management development used to be a peripheral activity for many firms. It has now sprung to centre stage, and internationalisation is one of the key reasons for its reassessment. As companies in widely differing industries demonstrate, firms must consider the fit between their international business objectives, their structure and their human resource policies. An organisation's employees will only keep pace with its international growth if these factors are regarded as an integrated whole.

Internationalisation has also resulted in a fundamental shift in management development focus. The traditional concentration on the individual will not build the kind of highly responsive international organisations that will be needed in future. Companies operating in the fast-moving and interdependent international markets of the 1990s will need to rely as never before on their capacity for promoting organisational learning and feedback across borders and on their ability to generate ownership of strategy across the organisation.

Management development must therefore contribute to the creation of a new corporate culture and a new managerial mind-set. It must aim to create an environment in which organisational learning can flourish and in which the worldwide organisation is involved in a continual search for improvement and for competitive advantage. Its task is to develop what Rhône-Poulenc calls "conviviality" among employees — in other words the ability to work together for the greater good of the organisation. This is why, as well as focusing on individual competences, management development must also focus on the collective competence of groups and so of the organisation as an whole.

THE INTERNATIONAL LEARNING ORGANISATION

The first essential is for the international company to grasp where its management development policies currently stand. Figure 5.1 is designed to help plot a firm's existing stance. The horizontal axis represents the status of management development in the organisation (in other words, how close management development is to the strategic concerns of the business.) The vertical axis is a continuum from highly individual management development to collective development.

Many firms are located in the lower left-hand quadrant of the model where management development is peripheral. Top management gives scant attention to it and sets little store by the counsel of human resource specialists. What management development does take place is ad hoc or accidental rather than planned. It focuses entirely on developing individual competences. Deceptively, this type of firm may actually be spending a great deal on such training,

Figure 5.1 **How does your company approach management development?**

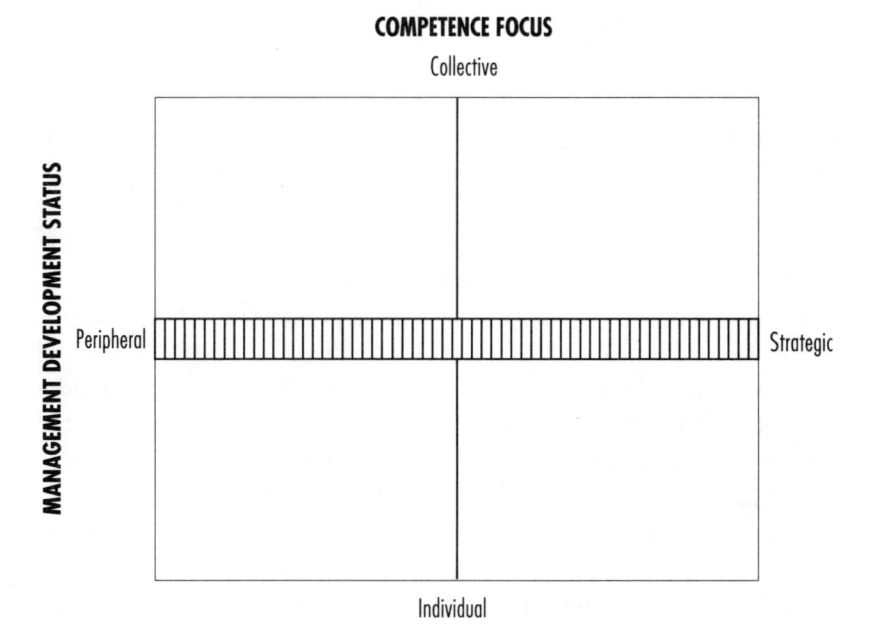

[Figure: A 2x2 matrix. Vertical axis labelled "MANAGEMENT DEVELOPMENT STATUS" ranging from "Peripheral" to "Strategic". Horizontal axis labelled "COMPETENCE FOCUS" ranging from "Individual" to "Collective".]

and may react indignantly to the charge that its management development policies are inappropriate or uncoordinated.

In contrast, in companies in the top right-hand quadrant the human resource and management development functions work closely with top management as part of the business team. Management development and training are closely related to business strategy. The emphasis here is on a continuous process that transforms individual learning, both "through the job" and "off the job", into organisational learning.

The other two quadrants of the diagram represent routes to the learning organisation. While there is little connection between management development and the fundamental policy of the business among companies in the top left-hand quadrant, there is some recognition that teamwork matters, and managers are encouraged to enhance their relationships with others as they carry out their functions. Firms in the bottom right-hand quadrant focus on the growth of the individual but relate this to the achievement of organisational goals at all levels of management. Management development here, however, may tend to concentrate on developing the people who will one day occupy the top posts.

The company which wants to survive and prosper in the global market place will aspire to be in the top right-hand quadrant – the international learning organisation. But how can a company develop into such an organisation? What steps are needed to ensure that management development both satisfies individual needs and helps the organisation to achieve its strategic priorities?

Centralisation versus decentralisation

A strategic approach to management development requires an organisation to take a worldwide view of its management resources. The main issue here is whether to pursue a centralised or decentralised approach. In decentralised multinational firms, responsibility for the early development of managers has been traditionally devolved to the subsidiaries. The corporate centre usually only becomes involved in the development of individuals when they start to assume more senior jobs or significant international responsibilities. In some firms now, however, the centre is taking greater interest in identifying and developing people much earlier in their careers. Ericsson, for example, has set up a worldwide system of management planning to enable it to tap the full management potential of the company. In an otherwise decentralised company, Rhône-Poulenc has also decided to carry out career planning on a worldwide basis. In giving more attention to integrating their international human resource efforts these companies are moving closer to Unilever, which believes that a centralised approach to management development is the best foundation for developing international managers.

The mechanism for establishing and maintaining a strategic perspective will vary from company to company and will partly depend on the firm's current approach to management development. Rhône-Poulenc, for example, set up an international human resources committee composed of corporate human resource executives and the national heads of human resources from its subsidiaries. Ericsson created its worldwide career planning system through a steering committee of top personnel managers and a series of task-forces made up of human resource people from all over the world. Electrolux, on the other hand, tries to avoid creating bureaucracy and prefers to maintain an informal dialogue between its human resource people around the world.

Whatever form the mechanism takes, two things are clear. First, top management involvement and commitment is essential. Sometimes the initiative for setting up such a system actually comes directly from top managers who understand that human resource policies are central to the process of internationalisation (as in the case of Fiat and Ericsson). In firms where the status of the management development function is peripheral, however, a close relationship between management development people and top managers does not exist. Here it becomes the task of human resource managers and development specialists to persuade their chief executive and senior line and functional managers that a strategic approach to management development is vital.

Second, taking a strategic view does not mean that head office can simply impose its ideas on its subsidiaries. Agreement on international human resource policies must be achieved through discussion and not by dictate. Companies like Rhône-Poulenc and Unilever strongly believe that the views of the overseas operating units must be respected. It is up to human resource staff at the centre to pay careful attention to their relationships with their counterparts in the subsidiaries and to promote a continuous dialogue with them. Integration is a subtly different process from centralisation.

Developing a strategy

Only when companies have resolved these knotty issues can they move on to the next logical step of creating an international learning organisation. A central concern here is how best to help managers acquire the international skills described in the previous chapter. From the answers to the Ashridge survey, it is evident that one of the most effective ways of developing international skills and perspectives is still by *direct* international experience "through the job", either by participation in international taskforces or, more importantly, through working and living abroad.

However, when these companies were asked how many of their managers currently have international experience and whether this was likely to increase, the answers showed that the proportion of managers with international experience ranged from 1 per cent (or even less) in some British firms to an exceptional 80 per cent in a Swiss firm. In many firms only 5–10 per cent of managers had international experience (although some firms indicated that the proportion of their high-flyers with such experience was likely to be greater).

Firms are clearly worried about the relatively low number of managers who have worked abroad. "This must and will change," said one UK organisation, and 69 per cent of the companies surveyed intend to increase the proportion of managers with international experience.

For the majority of these firms, developing their international management talent will demand considerable effort and commitment. The results of management development are difficult to measure in a domestic context. In the international arena, measurement presents other dilemmas. A resolute belief in the central role of management development in creating the international company is therefore needed.

How can a firm ensure that international experience is part of a carefully formulated strategy and not just something that is done because it seems a good idea? Unfocused international experience will be wasted unless it is part of a *planned* programme based on a consideration of what will be of real benefit to the individual and to the company. One firm said:

> "If this is not clear, then international experience should not happen. Even when it is beneficial to give someone international experience, this is often gained at considerable financial cost to the company and personal cost to the individual manager and his or her family. One must always ask: is this the best or only way to develop international skills?"

The elite versus the general

Another issue that companies have to tackle is the question of who should be given the opportunity to acquire international experience. Should international management development focus on creating an internationally skilled elite of high-potential managers? Or should it encompass a wider group of so-called "average" managers who nonetheless form the backbone of the organisation? Some companies feel that improving the skills of all managers even by a modest amount is much more beneficial than focusing exclusively on a small group of high-flyers. Advocates of such an approach argue that concentrating on an elite cadre risks creating an international spirit only at the top of the organisation.

Closely allied to the issue of who should be given international experience is the question of whether subsidiaries in other countries should be run by local or expatriate managers. The latter option tended to be the one most favoured by companies in the past, but many companies now believe that it is desirable for subsidiaries to be run by local managers. "Company policy is to have management of local origin in all countries," said a Danish firm in the Ashridge survey. A German company commented: "We will only fill a job vacancy abroad with an expatriate if a local person is not available, cannot be developed or cannot be hired on the open market." A UK company explained: "We have moved from the use of expatriates towards a mixture of locally employed managers and managers based in head office who travel widely. Locally employed managers are more knowledgeable and more stable."

There is, however, the problem that local managers often tend to create "baronies" or "fiefdoms". These prevent precisely that flow of information and co-operation that will be increasingly critical for the international firm. In addition, a policy of employing local managers reduces the opportunities for giving other managers international experience.

Short-term costs and long-term benefits

The decision about who to send abroad of course involves cost considerations. A commitment to international management development requires considerable investment in both time and money, and additionally requires considerable, often complex, administration. "Installing proper, professionally trained people to handle the administrative nightmares of moving people around the world" is a major challenge for many firms. The return on the investment is difficult to assess. Ultimately, it has to be an act of faith that the long-term pay-off in terms of an internationally more cohesive and effective organisation will justify the expenditure.

Trading off long-term benefits against short-term costs is an unavoidable necessity. In particular, companies have to accept the trade-off between maintaining short-term operational effectiveness and fulfilling long-term international development needs. We discovered that the way companies select managers for international assignments throws light on how they handle the potential conflict between the two. Participating companies in the Ashridge survey were asked to identify the most important criteria for choosing managers for international postings in their organisations. Contrast their answers in Table 5.1 (see page 103) with their views on the desirable characteristics of international managers as shown in Table 4.1 (see page 69). Although in the latter case "soft" personal qualities were valued as an ideal, "hard" technical skills win out when it actually comes to choosing managers for jobs abroad. Table 5.1 shows that the short-term requirements of the overseas job itself and the individual's technical expertise take precedence over management development objectives. Clearly many firms try to take account of

Table 5.1 **How are managers selected for international postings?**
(% of respondents ranking a factor as among the five most important selection criteria in their organisation)

	%
Technical skill/expertise for the job	85
Potential of manager to develop in role	69
Knowledge of company systems, procedures, etc	63
Understanding the market and customers	48
Appropriate language skills	46
Necessary component of career path	46
Support of spouse and family	38
Knowledge/understanding of culture/norms of the host country	25
Good health	13
Age	8
Seniority	6
Gender	2
Proven expatriate track record	2

Source: The Ashridge survey, 1989–90.

the individual's potential to develop in the role, but this is very often a subsidiary factor, which is also indicated by the relatively low ranking of international experience as a necessary qualification.

Sending a good manager abroad may also threaten the performance of the unit that they are leaving, as in the case of the firm which said that it finds it very difficult to release people from their present jobs.

Length of postings

Another particularly difficult aspect of the short-term/long-term dilemma emerged from the Ashridge survey when the length of international postings was discussed. This revealed anxieties about the length of time that it takes for someone to become effective in a job abroad.

For a start, it seems that international jobs are likely to be shorter when they are seen as development opportunities, as in the case of one British company which said it planned to use an increasing number of 1–2 year postings for development purposes, "rather than to fill vacancies as previously". Various other British firms also pointed to the increasing use of shorter, temporary assignments such as 3–6 month project postings.

In contrast, firms which are relatively new to the international scene, or which are putting greater emphasis on international expansion, expected international postings to be longer. "The length is probably increasing to 3–4 years to give people an opportunity to show results," said a Danish firm. One of the few British firms expecting longer postings said: "Contracts are tending to lengthen after three years because of the key nature of the roles performed."

Concern about the time that it takes for a manager to become effective in a post was reflected by a US company which said: "In the last few years, we offered two-year postings, sometimes three. Now it is shifting to 3–5 years. This is due to the recognition that a manager who is in a country longer gains more respect and makes a longer impact overall." Japanese firms agree. One of them said: "Short-term postings do not provide enough time for people to become familiar with the country."

Finnish companies, which are among the most internationally ambitious, are notably keen to give managers longer overseas postings so that they can build solid relationships with local customers. One Finnish company was worried about the use of short-term temporary assignments. "A period shorter than a year is useless," it declared. Another Finnish firm felt that even two years "is too short and too expensive to get true customer contacts". This company is therefore moving to 3–5 year contracts for its expatriate managers.

A Dutch company that took part in the survey pointed to another problem. International postings, it said, "are getting longer because a shortage of managers willing to travel means that those who are willing tend to stay longer". This company expressed a fear that people's unwillingness to travel was going to be a major challenge for its international aspirations. What is the source of this reluctance?

The international manager or the international family?

The surveyed companies were asked about the willingness of their managers to go abroad. Some 38 per cent thought that managers are more willing than they were to accept international postings. This stems from enthusiasm generated by 1992 or because "people's perceptions of jobs abroad are not so narrow today," according to one UK company. However, a significant 25 per cent of companies felt that their managers are less willing to go. These companies indicated various reasons for this reluctance. Fears about children's education and dual career situations came top of the list, as shown in Table 5.2.

Concern about family mobility is an increasing constraint. One company said: "People are more choosy about location and timing. They are quite likely to turn down a foreign posting because of family reasons such as children's schooling or the wife's job." Even where managers are willing to go abroad, their spouses may be less willing to disturb family life. One US firm noted: "People are generally less willing to disrupt personal lives just because the company requests it." Another said: "The whole family has to buy into the idea."

Faced with these constraints, it may well be more logical to consider whether to send younger managers abroad. After all, younger managers tend to have fewer family ties. The evidence from

Table 5.2 **What stops companies giving international experience to managers?**
(% of respondents who ranked a factor as among the five most important constraints in their organisation)

	%
Disruption of children's education	77
Spouse/partner reluctant to give up own career	67
Fear of losing influence/visibility at corporate centre	54
Organisation finds difficulty in re-absorbing returning managers	52
Lack of co-ordinated approach across the company	48
Managers find reintegration difficult on return	31
Immigration/employment laws and host country restrictions	29
Financial constraints	29
Lack of perceived need	19
Elderly relatives	17
Host country subsidiaries unwilling to accept managers	8
Subsidiaries in non-parent countries unwilling to release managers	8

Source: The Ashridge survey, 1989–90.

the survey however suggests that many firms are not prepared to give their managers real experience of living and working in other countries until they reach the ranks of middle management. One firm said that giving international experience to junior managers is too risky; it preferred to wait until they were committed. A German company emphasised that managers sent abroad "must have a knowledge of our product range and our business philosophy" and that such a thorough understanding takes time to develop.

The irony is that by the time people reach middle management, family-related issues often impede mobility and firms can expect people to be much more fussy about location and benefits.

Many companies which try to provide junior people with international exposure mainly do so through what they perceive as less risky methods such as meetings; visits to plants and offices; international conferences; work projects and specific learning assignments; and management or language-training courses. In future they may have to be bolder, particularly as many of their recruits will be looking for positive evidence that the company offers international career paths.

The Hongkong and Shanghai Bank training programme

This is an issue that has very much been taken to heart by the Hongkong and Shanghai Banking Corporation. Like many multinational companies, it has a dual career structure. It recruits graduates who choose to be international officers and who will eventually be posted to any of the bank's operations worldwide. Other graduates are recruited as resident officers and their career track will generally be within their own country.

Both sets of graduates undergo the six-month executive trainee development programme, which provides a mixture of technical and interpersonal skills as well as a range of opportunities to develop cultural sensitivity and build cultural synergy. The programme draws participants from all over the world and it is not unusual for as many as ten different nationalities to be working and living closely together for the first six months of their banking career.

An executive trainer at the bank observes: "This international peer group has great advantages in that it enables trainees to observe, discuss and understand each other; to work through conflict; and to operate as a team during the course of their initial training. Business and social contacts made in the first six months often last a lifetime."

The training programme is divided into four phases. In stage one, the initial orientation and team-building process takes place during a two-day cultural awareness seminar designed by Sara Tang, principal lecturer in human resource management in the Department of Business and Management at the City Polytechnic of Hong Kong, and Paul Kirkbride, British Aerospace Professor of Organisation Development at the Hartfield Polytechnic Business School in the UK. The aim of the programme is to understand how participants' cultural background shapes their values, attitudes and subsequent behaviour and thus the way they are perceived by people from other cultures.

The second phase of the executive trainee programme consists of a ten-day outdoor personal development course, which provides "a live opportunity to explore cultural differences and build greater synergy and team identity". Held in Hong Kong's rural New Territories, the course provides participants with experience of such "overt and direct cultural differences as eating habits, attitudes towards privacy, cleanliness and dress. They also have to come to terms with more abstract and implicit cultural differences in areas such as participation, trust and interpersonal relations." On return, the participants undergo a week-long interpersonal skills development course as phase three of the programme.

The final stage of the programme is an international assignment. This gives trainees the opportunity both to gain initial experience in one of the bank's branches and of working in a culture different from their own. "This reinforces the cross-cultural learning from the initial sensitivity training, peer group experience and skills training. Attachments may not be to the country of initial posting because the aim is to foster cross-cultural awareness and sensitivity, not simply specific culture knowledge."[1]

INTERNATIONAL CAREER PLANNING

To achieve greater international mobility throughout the organisation, companies will have to give much more systematic attention to international career planning. In the next section of this chapter, some examples are given of just a few of the many approaches that have been adopted by a variety of international firms.

The Unilever programme

Few firms approach the level of mobility to be found in Unilever, where the need to ensure international movement throughout the organisation is an article of faith.

Unilever's approach to management development is founded on the belief that people need a broad experience in a changing world and that part of the breadth of experience is acquired by moving them around different countries. It is also keen to avoid limiting people to only one product group.

At any one time there are around 1,000 Unilever managers working outside their home country. An average spell abroad lasts about four years, so by the time people get near to the top of the company the majority have worked in other countries and also in companies that themselves have a mix of nationalities. "If you don't develop a respect for other cultures in that situation, then you are brain dead," suggests David Jones, Unilever's head of training.

Tony Vineall, the company's director of personnel, responsible for worldwide management development, identifies another, but not often appreciated, aspect of international experience. You can have someone, he says, who may have successfully run plants in the UK, Nigeria, Colombia and the USA. "You can hardly say he is lacking in international experience, but in a sense he still could be, if he had not had to run something in two or more places at the same time." Responsibility for developing policies and achieving results in more than one culture at the same time is an essential part of Unilever's approach.

Unilever describes its career planning system as "short-term succession planning but long-term talent planning". Its worldwide guidelines stipulate that the wide range of Unilever product groups and countries should be used to develop the expertise of individual managers. Not everyone will work everywhere, but it will be unusual in future for young managers of potential to stay more than 5–6 years in one company or country. Those who reach the top jobs must have worked outside their own country at least once.

Unilever regards it as crucial that management development at any stage should both train and test individuals. The process of assessing potential should take place simultaneously with the development process. Careers should also include exposure to the full range of different kinds of experience within a function so that managers will eventually be ready to take up posts as heads of functions on company boards. For example, marketing managers should have sales experience and personnel managers should have factory and industrial relations experience and also work on management development and training.

The guidelines also lay down that careers should include, wherever possible, early experience of responsibility for achieving results. Planned experience must be supplemented by formal training. All managers have a formal annual appraisal when performance against the job is reviewed and discussed with their manager.

Unilever is very clear that these policies have important implications for how the business is run and the way that it tries to reconcile short-term business priorities with longer-term management development needs. Every job must be considered both as a job to be done and as an opportunity to develop someone's expertise. Organisation structures must include jobs of the right level and size to provide sensible "stepping stones" in careers and some jobs must contain elements of higher-level jobs to train and test people with potential.

Unilever's organisation structures may also have to "bend" to accommodate and challenge people who are being developed for bigger jobs later. Furthermore, risks must be taken – "procrastination is a fatal flaw", says the company. An enormous amount of time must also be devoted to planning, reviewing and counselling.

Such guidelines aim to ensure that talent is being attracted and nurtured wherever Unilever operates; and the operators in those countries are continuously involved in their development.

Assessment is carried out within the framework of development lists ("talent-spotting lists"). The company divides its management jobs into four levels and maintains a central list of people in each business and each country who could have the potential to move to each level within five years. Much of senior management's time is invested in reviewing the lists to ensure both their continuing validity and that people are receiving the appropriate experience. Each overseas region reviews its overall resource situation with the personnel division, and in each country a national planning committee looks at the overall supply and demand position. Finally, there is an overall review carried out by the top Special Committee (including the joint chairmen) and the personnel division when policies and plans are adjusted. This forms the background for all the appointments made in the following year. When job vacancies are considered, the development needs of "listers" receive special consideration.

Tony Vineall says that Unilever's common international systems of job classification, potential assessment and categorisation of current performance are not "particularly special" in themselves but "the fact that they are widely understood and totally accepted is an important foundation of what we do".

He emphasises that ensuring diversity of experience for people has to be weighed against the operational needs of the business and against such considerations as people being in the job "long enough to learn from their mistakes".

Mobility at Rhône-Poulenc

Against a background of rapid global expansion, Rhône-Poulenc is placing increasing emphasis on the need to move its managers around. By 1995 it wants to have two tiers of managers with international experience, to become *jeunes sans frontières*, who can "forget the notion of nationality" and help build a truly global company.

The company has 420 expatriates working in 65 countries around the world for an average of four years. Five years ago it had only 250 managers on international assignments, most of them French. Today 275 of the expatriates are French, while the remaining 145 come from 16 different countries.

In strategic terms, Rhône-Poulenc has clear reasons for wanting more managers to pursue international careers. They include:

- The company has transformed itself rapidly into a global business. Moving managers between different countries is one way of helping all employees to become aware of the geographical and industrial spread of the company's activities.

- Moving managers around the group helps integrate new businesses. The company realises that face-to-face contact between managers of the new businesses and Rhône-Poulenc employees, senior managers in particular, is a valuable way of helping the newcomers feel part of the group. This is important in a business that places great emphasis on *esprit de corps*.
- International assignments aid the flow of information, both about technical matters and market requirements.
- Rhône-Poulenc must have some way of ensuring that managers, whether based in France or Brazil, are not locked into national insularity but gain a comprehensive understanding of the group as a whole. International career development is one way of ensuring that the company has a pool of such people who may one day hold senior positions within the group.

Recognising that, in a sense, it was entering a whole new ball-game in career planning, the group established the Comité International des Ressources Humaines (International Human Resources Committee) in 1988. A firm believer in decentralisation, the group allows its national managers to take responsibility for human resources and management development. Breaking with tradition, however, it decided that international career planning had to be done on a worldwide basis.

The committee is composed of human resource people and the national heads of human resources and its remit was to establish group-wide policies and procedures for handling international assignments. A comprehensive framework now exists which details conditions of employment for expatriates working in different countries, including advice on the most appropriate arrangements for pensions, remuneration, housing and so on. The group stresses that this is a guideline; it is left to national managers to use it as they think appropriate in their local circumstances.

The committee has now moved to a new stage of international human resource management. It is concentrating on the whole issue of international career management from the stage of graduate recruitment onwards. It has worked on a number of initiatives: recruiting graduates for an international career; encouraging and facilitating a greater number of international assignments for high-potential, young managers; and considering ways of building more international content into existing development programmes.

The simple benefit of bringing managers of different nationalities together as early as possible is also becoming apparent to Rhône-Poulenc. At the moment it runs a two-week course for new French managers, about 350–400 each year, to introduce them to the group. Managers outside France do not have a similar course, and the group is now considering creating a programme for them. Getting around language differences is a problem, however, and the group may start in a small way by simply including French-speaking foreign managers in the present programme, or starting a new, English-speaking course. Blain concludes: "Whatever we do, we want to encourage new managers from all over the world to mix together. It is important to create relationships so that managers at every level know each other and can work together."

GrandMet: A systematic approach

GrandMet, the UK-based international food, drinks and retailing business, is another company that believes that developing international managers requires a systematic approach. It is taking steps to ensure that all its businesses throughout the world have experienced international managers in place. It wants to avoid drawing too much on UK or US managers and is convinced that to achieve this goal it is necessary to take an interventionist approach to career planning. Alan Wild, GrandMet's director of employment policy explains:

> "The normal processes of selection and development are not very efficient at producing international managers. Developing people internationally will generally not meet short-term business objectives in two ways. First, you may not pick the best person for a particular vacancy from the point of view of immediate performance. Secondly, moving a high-potential individual into a post which will provide international experience may not be the move that will allow him or her to make the maximum short-term contribution to the business."

Developing international managers, therefore, calls for active intervention in people's careers. "Both the company and the individual have to agree to mortgage short-term considerations." International Vintners & Distillers, one of GrandMet's major businesses, has taken such an interventionist approach through an international management development programme which it started in 1988. Called the "cadre" programme, it aims to send young managers of high potential on international assignments before ultimately placing them in senior management positions in their home countries.

IDV hopes that in the long term the programme will help to internationalise its management structure. Currently, although there are a large number of non-UK managers in the company's top 200 managerial jobs, not very many of these have experience of managing outside their own country. By the end of this decade the cadre programme should help to create a pool of internationally experienced national managers who will be capable of assuming the top jobs.

One of the great benefits of the programme is that it is a means of giving international experience to managers at a much earlier stage of their careers. IDV would not have considered sending junior or middle managers overseas before because of the risks and expenses involved. Since the company's policy has always been to recruit locally and to develop local managers whenever possible, it has never had, indeed has never wanted to have, a large pool of expatriate senior managers. The concept of the cadre programme, by contrast, fits more comfortably with the philosophy of decentralisation as its ultimate aim is for the participants to return eventually to their home countries.

IDV's director of management development and training, Linda Clayton, stresses that the programme is not an elaborate "galactic trial" for future leaders, or an exclusive "crown prince" programme. "Although we want people with potential, we do not presume to predict how far they will eventually go – it is too difficult to judge. We simply want to broaden managers."

While cadre managers are perceived as different at IDV, "they are not seen as an elite. They are very dispersed throughout the company, so no blocks or cliques can be seen. Any one country only has two or three such people."

In total, around 12–15 managers go through the cadre programme at any given time. Those who are selected tend to be 25–30 years of age, a time of life when people are mobile and are more willing to consider frequent career moves, IDV believes. They are sent on a maximum of four assignments, each of them lasting around 18–24 months. The majority of managers are not away from their home country for any longer than six years as the company is keen for them to apply their newly acquired international perspective to local markets.

Managers are recruited for the programme both from inside and outside IDV. They undergo a rigorous selection process, using a combination of assessment methods and personal recommendations. The company also uses an "international assignment inventory", based on a questionnaire, to assess any traits and skills which it believes are particularly linked to success abroad, such as flexibility, cultural sensitivity and the ability to integrate. The inventory also tries to flush out any prejudices that might hinder a manager from adjusting to an unfamiliar culture.

During selection interviews, IDV is primarily looking for career motivation and a willingness to live in different conditions. In terms of technical skills, IDV is seeking managers who have built up credibility within the organisation and who have the intellectual ability to "get up to speed quickly in the new market place". "Our business is very much about relationships and brand management. The core capabilities of IDV managers are being able to perceive what brands are all about and being able to develop the right kind of relationships with our customers and business partners."

Young managers with all these traits are obviously few and far between, something which became quickly apparent to IDV when it began recruiting for the programme. GrandMet's Alan Wild comments: "Many of those most interested in taking time out to travel did not have the ability, potential and maturity. Their reasons for wanting a series of international moves were not primarily motivated out of building a successful career."

Now that people understand the programme better, IDV's Linda Clayton says a large degree of self-selection comes into play. Many managers consider the programme even more carefully in the face of the undeniable career risks involved in moving into an unfamiliar culture and business environment. Wild points out:

> "The 25-year-old high-flyer is generally doing 'very nicely thank you'. He or she often has a clear view of how their career could develop in the home country. This is often reinforced by their boss. The cadre can be seen as an extremely risky four to six-year pause in the upward tracking of their professional career. This is particularly true for professionals moving into what are perceived as less advanced economies."

IDV holds frank and extensive discussions about the pros and cons of the cadre with the potential participant, some of whom may have been first approached by the company itself. It also allows the manager and his or her family to visit the placement country before any form of commitment is made. The wisdom of both sides holding realistic expectations about the programme was underlined to IDV when the programme first started. The company assigned a Latin American manager to a joint venture in Switzerland. At that stage it did not use the overseas assignment inventory or send people in advance of a posting to the placement company so they could learn about the country and some of the cultural issues they might encounter.

> "When taken to the flat on arrival in Switzerland, this manager looked around and asked where the maid was going to sleep. They were used to this standard at home – it hadn't occurred to them that this wouldn't be laid on in Switzerland. It certainly hadn't occurred to us that they would expect a maid. At that stage we simply didn't check for these type of situations; we just didn't think of them at the time."

There is no question that the cadre programme represents a considerable investment for GrandMet and IDV. IDV is unlikely to reap the full benefits of the programme for some years to come. It estimates that the pay-back of having more internationally experienced managers will only start in 8–10 years' time, when the cadre assignees begin to reach senior positions within IDV. It is well aware that a degree of speculation is involved; cadre managers could of course take their valuable international know-how elsewhere. It is still too early to compile data about the rate of retention, but it is nevertheless optimistic that cadre managers will stay with the group. "The degree of commitment among participants is very high."

Important lessons

GrandMet and IDV have learned some important first principles about developing international managers:

- Don't be over-ambitious. Companies that don't have administrative systems for international postings already in place should think very seriously before embarking on a full-scale international management development programme of this sort.
- Gain top management support. For any international programme to succeed it is vital that everyone in the organisation knows that top management views it as strategically important and a worthwhile investment.
- Be flexible. Any form of rigidity will condemn the initiative to failure. If both the company and the individual are to get maximum benefit, the programme should be organised as flexibly as possible.
- Have a strategic direction so that you know what you are aiming towards and you can assess whether you have chosen the best route. Strategic clarity will also enable an organisation to deal with the complex trade-offs between commercial reality and individual development needs.
- Be realistic about expectations. Avoid letting managers think they are in a "crown prince" scenario.
- Emphasise to managers the career risk involved in going to work in an unfamiliar environment.

Starting with the subsidiaries at Ericsson

As it expanded internationally, Ericsson rapidly reached the conclusion that, as far as it was concerned, management development poli-

could not be dictated from the centre. They needed to start within the subsidiaries. Britt Reigo, senior vice-president for corporate human resources and organisation, has been the central figure in the development of Ericsson's approach to international management development. The company had carried out management planning at the corporate level for many years, but it had taken an ad hoc approach to management succession elsewhere in the organisation. Reigo says: "I realised very soon that it was impossible to sit here at the centre and work on management planning. It had to start with the subsidiaries."

The decision to set up a system that could more effectively tap the company's international talent was taken at the very top of the organisation. Under the guidance of a steering committee, composed of business area personnel and chaired by Reigo, a number of taskforces were set up, each made up of four or five human resource managers from all over the world, to consider the different issues involved. These included: the desired profile and skills of managers, candidate identification, key positions, career development, and control and systems. (The leadership model that resulted from the work of the first of these taskforces and which forms the basis of the career planning system was described in Chapter 4.)

The result has been the introduction of a system that is based on a clear identification of Ericsson's needs, that is very straightforward in its application, and that can be applied around the world.

Top managers are selected through an annual review process. The chief executive and the senior vice-president for human resources and organisation review management plans in the light of the firm's strategic plans. The chief executive of each of the six business areas reports on the candidates for upper management positions in their area, as well as on plans for each candidate's training and education. Before this, similar reviews are carried out at the various levels within each business area.

Lower down the organisation, management planning begins at department level within subsidiaries, where department managers and their immediate superiors review potential candidates for more qualified and responsible positions. Annual appraisals are made in co-operation with other managers and sometimes with the personnel department. The manager also verifies them with his or her immediate superior.

The next stage is a report from the manager to a management planning meeting at either division or company level. After discussion, the meeting decides which candidates will be offered the opportunity to enter a management development programme.

Only after the candidate has accepted the offer does work begin on the development of an individual development plan, whose design and execution is the responsibility of the candidate and his or her immediate superior. All development plans have to be approved, however, by the personnel manager responsible for the department or by the management planning meeting.

Combining centralisation with decentralisation at Accor

Accor has adopted an approach to international career planning that combines decentralised and centralised methods. The company estimates that by the end of the decade it will have nearly 100,000 employees through organic growth alone. On average, the group is recruiting 4,500 employees a year. This poses something of a logistics headache in a group that wants to promote international mobility.

Accor has decided that for more junior positions decentralised selection works best. Local managers are expected to define the job content and behavioural requirements of positions that are not strategically important – that is jobs that do not have a direct impact on either brand or corporate results. The group is undeterred by the likelihood that local managers will base their decisions on different selection criteria. "The corporate centre tells our people what the overall strategy is and leaves them to work out what they need," says Volker Büring, Accor's vice-president for human resources.

Key positions, including middle and senior management positions, are the responsibility of the corporate centre. A top priority has been to find ways of comparing key jobs so that high-potential managers can be moved between different brands and divisions. "Success in international career planning depends on whether highly diverse jobs can be compared using the same criteria."

Accor has developed a system of evaluation that can be applied through all the brands and divisions. The majority of key strategic positions, about 450, have been clearly defined, using job requirement profiles stored in a computer database. The records of the qualifications and skills of high-potential managers allow the matching of individuals to jobs and also expose gaps in the organisation where vital skills are lacking or are underdeveloped.

Electrolux subsidiaries chart their own route

In line with its anti-bureaucratic philosophy, Electrolux does not have well-established, centrally controlled systems of career progression. This partly stems from the fact that the parent group believes the local companies are quite capable of handling their human resources issues without too much interference from head office. It would like to see more of its managers gain experience of working abroad, but it wants to avoid "sending the wrong message" and giving local companies the impression that Swedes are dictating policy. Electrolux hopes, rather, that a developing "consciousness" will lead to the desired exchanges.

In the longer term, Electrolux feels that, if it is to become a truly global corporation, it will be essential to bring more non-Swedish managers into the ranks of its senior and top management.

The pragmatic approach at Varity

Varity, the North American-based industrial management company that embraces tractor manufacturer Massey Ferguson and Perkins, the engineering company, is another group that does not see the need for a formal, centralised management development programme. It has adopted a rather more pragmatic approach. The company is certainly spreading its wings globally, but it never forgets that what it does best is running an engineering operation.

This means that there is no special international human resource approach at corporate level. Instead the company does the things that need to be done to develop good managers at all levels and if some of these are in an international context, then their form will be affected appropriately. As Alan Don, vice-president for organisation and executive planning, puts it: "If you start with thinking about international management development rather than with thinking first about the company's business needs, its strategy and structure, and its human resource policies, you're seeing the flower without the seed."

The company does not therefore give a lot of attention to ensuring that its managers are culture-sensitive in the abstract sense. It is more concerned that they should be sensitive to their environments and the people with whom they deal. It has not set itself the aim of equipping every one of its managers with a global perspective, but rather of equipping those who go abroad with what they need for their own circumstances. For example, only when someone is going to work in another country will the company provide a total immersion language programme, which will be immediately applicable to that person's situation.

Succession planning and career development drive management development at Varity. These are based on long-term perspectives so that the company is not continually pulling people up by the roots to see how they are growing. Thus people will not be shifted internationally merely for developmental purposes.

Management development takes place within Varity's three business groups, with the corporate headquarters taking a keen interest in the top appointments in each of the businesses within the groups. Each group vice-president is responsible for maintaining the organisation and management strength of the group, reporting annually to the chairman/CEO and president of Varity Corporation the organisation and succession plans for the first line in his or her business. The vice-president makes recommendations on major significant organisation changes to the business and all appointments at general manager level and is also involved in all appointments affecting the first line to the general manager. The strength of the group is seen to depend pre-eminently on the quality of the general managers of the individual businesses and is one of the methods that Varity headquarters uses to measure the performance of the group vice-president.

One of the most important factors in assessing managers' potential at Varity is the "capacity curve" – the ability of people to handle greater numbers of variables as they progress in their careers. Some general managers' capability does not go beyond running a small business; some are capable of managing a very large business. The critical factor is the size of the organisation, not whether it is international, says Alan Don.

Varity demonstrates quite powerfully that there can be no single approach to international management development – each approach must be determined by the nature and context of the business. For Varity there is only the broadest emphasis on international management development as a separate activity. Managers are expected to do a good job where they are in their current environment. From that performance they may be able to move to greater things which are likely to contain more global responsibility. If they do well they get picked up by the formal planning process. Varity's essentially pragmatic outlook is a salutary reminder that whatever an organisation does in terms of "internationalising" its business, it must be driven by real business need.

Benchmarks and objectives

Every company will devise its own model of international career planning to suit its own specific needs at its current stage of development. However, several benchmarks and objectives have emerged from our discussions with international companies that are clearly important in all circumstances. These are summarised in the checklist which follows.

INTERNATIONAL CAREER PLANNING CHECKLIST

- Managers who are promoted to top management should have worked outside their own country at least once.
- Local managers appointed to run a subsidiary should have worked outside their own country, including a spell at the corporate centre.
- Staff from the corporate centre should also be given experience of working abroad.
- Opportunities for international experience and exposure should be provided for young recruits.
- International appointments must be seen as *both* a job to be done *and* as an opportunity to develop someone.
- International assignments should be seen *both* as opportunities to develop individuals *and* to develop the organisation by promoting the internal information flow.

- Organisation structures must "stretch" to allow opportunities for managers to gain international experience.
- Companies should regard managers and their families as one unit in terms of preparation for an international posting and where benefits and conditions are concerned. The family has earning power as a unit and should be compensated as such.
- The benefits of planned international experience should be augmented by formal management education programmes.
- Top management support and commitment to a policy of international management development is crucial.
- The people who are expected to implement the system, especially the local human resource staff, must be fully involved in its planning.

The creation of the international learning organisation depends heavily on approaches to international management development that build not only on individual competence but also on the organisation's collective competence.

In the global arena, management development and organisation development go hand in hand. One of the major tasks is to build a collective learning environment which promotes a sharing of experience and development on a worldwide scale and which fosters an easy dialogue between the different countries and cultures that a company encompasses. The future is not just about international competition or international collaboration; it is also about international learning. Managing across borders means learning across borders. As the ancient prophet said: "Many shall run to and fro, and knowledge shall be increased."

Reference

1 P. Hawthorne, S. Tang and P. Kirkbride, "Creating the culturally sensitive Hongkong Bank manager", *EMD Journal*, (European Foundation for Management Development), no. 4, 1990, pp. 14-17.

CHAPTER 6

RECRUITING INTERNATIONALLY

The market for management talent will be intensely competitive throughout the 1990s, despite recessionary interludes. Demographic trends mean a sharp decline in the number of young people in the developed economies, and skill shortages will put companies under further pressure. This pincer movement has already effected a radical change in companies' recruitment strategies. Leading firms now acknowledge that they can no longer rely solely on their "home" labour markets. If they are to remain competitive, companies must tap into new sources of labour to find the best people at the most competitive price.

Vlad Stanic, head of management development for the UK bank, TSB Group plc, points out that British companies are exploring a host of unconventional ways to reduce the shortfall in their recruitment targets. These new approaches include launching recruitment drives in neglected sectors of the labour market; female staff, second-career managers, ethnic minorities and the disabled. "Within this context, recruitment forays into the international market place are proving better value and more cost effective."[1]

The motive to recruit internationally, however, goes beyond concern about labour shortages and rising employment costs. International recruitment is also being driven by companies' desire to create a more international ethos in their organisations. Unilever, for instance, emphasises the importance of having a mix of cultural perspectives in an operation to prevent people thinking too narrowly.

Finding people with international skills is no easy matter. And where such candidates are found, companies will almost certainly find their rivals fighting over the same pool of talent. It is hardly surprising, therefore, that firms are taking the initiative and tackling the problem in a different way. If a commodity is rare, it is logical to produce it yourself, if possible.

The hunt for the internationally oriented graduate is not confined to European companies. Procter & Gamble, the US consumer products giant, placed a full-page advertisement in *The Economist* in November 1990 inviting top engineering students across Europe to the first Euro Technical Management Seminar, which was held at the company's Italian headquarters in Rome. With the evident aim of flushing out some of Europe's brightest engineering undergraduates ahead of rival firms, 25 students were offered "the opportunity to enter the real business world and develop management skills working with Procter & Gamble executives through case studies drawn from our experience". The company offered to pay travel and accommodation expenses to successful applicants who lived up to the following pre-requisites: qualities of leadership; an outstanding academic record; graduating in 1991 or 1992; and a good knowledge of English.

General Electric considers itself a pioneer in global recruitment approaches. It has had a good grasp of the US recruitment scene for many years, but it is now slowly learning how to recruit elsewhere in the world. It has integrated its MBA and PhD recruitment worldwide and is trying to integrate its batchelor degree-level recruitment as a partnership between the company and its businesses.

GE tries to ensure that in their first 3–5 years in the company young recruits develop "global brains" very quickly. Some of the individual businesses have arranged job-rotation, job-swapping or job-shadowing schemes. There are also corporate programmes involving job-rotation and training in some functional areas such as manufacturing and finance. GE would like eventually to be able to globalise the programmes so that people could join them from anywhere in the world and have at least one assignment outside their country of origin.

Olivetti's "No Frontiers" campaign

Probably the most ambitious pan-European recruitment drive has been launched by Olivetti, the Italian computer company. Its "No Frontiers" campaign is aimed at recruiting 1,000 specialists from which the company hopes to develop a pool of talented young managers with the potential to become top managers. Olivetti has run a worldwide advertising campaign entirely in English. Recruiters in the individual subsidiaries were all carefully trained by headquarters instructors to look for the same qualities in candidates and to give them the same emphasis. All successful candidates were then flown in to undergo the "No Frontiers" programme at the company's headquarters at Ivrea in Italy. The company has succeeded in obtaining a diverse range of nationalities; the third intake of graduates, for example, included 13 different nationalities in a group of 58 individuals.

This intensive programme includes two six-month periods of on-the-job training. One result is the formation of personal networks between participants. "Candidates form a strong personal network," says Tirad Sorooshian, Olivetti's UK international projects training manager. "Back at their jobs, they phone each other to talk over problems and help each other."[2]

Cross-border recruitment; the IBM experience

Cross-border recruitment is not, however, without its difficulties, even for firms with international experience, as IBM Europe discovered when it recently considered ways of promoting greater career mobility by moving away from nationally based recruitment policies to a more integrated and international approach.

Although the company has a well-developed international product development strategy, it has traditionally favoured a strategy of selling nationally. Recruitment has therefore been organised on a national basis, with IBM companies recruiting for their own local businesses. IBM Europe now wants to achieve greater internationalisation and to overcome the constraints on mobility posed by national recruiting.

In 1989 the company started to investigate the possibility of introducing a European employment contract for its graduate recruits. The idea was that, after being recruited and given initial training in their home country, recruits would be sent to another European country for two or three years. The newly hired employees would receive the same terms and conditions as other employees in the working country and it was expected that they would easily become part of the community. "The idea was to make these people Europeans and mobile from day one."

Unfortunately, there were legal obstacles. The much-discussed European Social Charter focuses on the basic protection of workers rather than the removal of impediments to mobility. While there is now a proposal for a European Company Statute, it will not replace local labour laws. The employee of a European Statute company will not be a European employee because the national labour legislation prevails. Even within a European Statute company, employees will remain under the jurisdiction of local law in each country. Other problems include the lack of pension portability and salary differentials between countries. While, for instance, French and German incomes are close when considering indirect and direct taxation, this is not the case in other countries such as the UK, Spain or Portugal.

IBM also found that an equally difficult problem is people's reluctance to move. The company carried out a survey of graduates' views about working abroad. This revealed some surprisingly conservative attitudes. IBM was disappointed to find that young people would be willing to work abroad as long as their spending power was protected. But they also wanted to be able to break their contracts and return home if they wished. They regarded working abroad as acceptable as long as they were single but felt that when they married they would need to establish themselves in their own country.

Despite the obstacles to mobility that it discovered, IBM feels that its research has been valuable in showing what is possible and in opening up the issues with local operating units. The company is now adopting a more gradual approach to moving away from nationalistic recruitment. It will continue to recruit more non-nationals for its local operations as long as they have the necessary qualifications, languages and the ability to relate to the customer. The company believes that people's attitudes towards working outside their own country will change, but slowly.

More barriers to cross-border recruitment

Other problems stem from the unwillingness of countries to accept qualifications gained elsewhere. There is also the difficulty of assessing the experience and qualifications of other nationals. While graduates in the UK qualify at the age of 21, for instance, those in Germany do so in their late 20s.

Richard Pearson, deputy director of the Institute of Manpower Studies in the UK, confirms that while 1992 will remove such barriers as the need for work permits, other problems will continue to hinder international recruitment. He suggests that a problem for British recruiters in particular will be tracking down graduates in other European countries.[3]

> "For example, while UK [university] career services help recruiters by 'selling' their graduates, in many parts of Europe such campus-based services are rare. In some cases direct recruitment is banned on campuses. Recruitment is mainly carried out through personal links with academics, student work-placements, direct advertising in newspapers and journals, and the national employment services."

A further problem, affecting virtually any business, is the difficulty of comparing the relative merits of institutions. How do you assess a graduate in comparison with one from Berlin or Barcelona? "All these factors suggest the need for a local presence to guide the recruitment process."

Unfamiliarity with local selection procedures presents obstacles to the would-be pan-European recruiter. Much research and preparation is needed in order to maintain the quality of recruitment while attuning it to the local situation. Incomes Data Services and the Institute of Personnel Management in the UK publish a helpful guide to recruitment practices in different European countries (Belgium, Denmark, France, Germany, Greece, Ireland, Italy, the Netherlands, Portugal and Spain). This provides, by country, an overview of recruitment conditions and the labour market; statutory provisions on workforce consultation; options other than full-time recruitment; how to find applicants through state employment agencies, employment agencies, headhunters, and advertising media; graduate recruitment; and the law and practice of selection, job offers and acceptance.[4]

Vlad Stanic of TSB stresses the problems of establishing the most appropriate remuneration and benefits packages when recruiting in the international market place. Career advancement and development prospects need even more careful attention.

"One of the difficulties in this respect is the compatibility of knowledge, skills and potential across different national and cultural types ... Managers experienced in the multinational environment will recognise the very real differences expressed through the stereotypes of the participative Scandinavian manager compared with the macho Latin counterpart. While there is evidence to suggest that these styles are converging, it is important to bear them in mind – especially when inducting recruits from one country in to a different working environment in another country."[5]

General Electric has also found it difficult to arrive at common assessment procedures for recruits from different cultures. One of the biggest knowledge gaps for many companies is understanding the expectations of young people in different countries. "We would not presume to know as much about what goes on in the mind of a young Japanese or a Hungarian as we would a young American."

Rhône-Poulenc's international career enticement

Some companies are undeterred by the problems of cross-border recruitment and feel that the offer of international experience will attract the right people. To attract as many high-flyers as possible from other countries, Rhône-Poulenc is offering graduates the enticement of an international career. "We decided that if they would not come to us, we would go to them," explains Roland Blain, a member of the human resources committee. The *Jeunes Cadres Internationaux* programme offers the opportunity of working as a manager in France, then working for a few years abroad.

Country representatives have the task of wooing students from whichever educational institutions they believe produce the best brains. In contrast to the IBM experience, they lure students with the promise of working abroad for 8–10 years. The young managers first attend the group's training centre at Cergy-Pontoise in France for five months to learn French, and about the organisation of the group and its four core businesses. At the end of this training they and the company decide in which section they would like to work.

"We deliberately avoid telling them what to do. It is very important to expose them to different possibilities and for them to choose the job that seems the most interesting." General managers help the graduates by meeting them personally and telling them about their job, division and product. The general manager may even offer the graduate a position to work alongside him or her. This process once again emphasises the importance of establishing networks of contacts.

Once assigned to a position the graduate works in France for 3–4 years, followed by two spells abroad, each lasting 2–4 years. By then the company is keen that they return to their home countries to work in a senior management position. The group particularly hopes that satisfaction with their international experience will attract their high-flying peers and friends to work for Rhône-Poulenc as well.

International recruitment at Accor

Another French group, the hotel company Accor, is trying to improve its hiring practices in order to reduce the industry-wide problem of high staff turnover and to recruit people who will be able to move and change along with the business. The group, which recruits 4,500 employees a year, is fast developing links with universities, business schools and hotel schools all over Europe. A booklet has been produced rather like a student-written "alternative prospectus", which discusses Accor's management style, career opportunities and anything else that might particularly attract students.

Accor has also revamped the training it offers to promising young graduates, mindful that these are people that virtually every blue-chip European company is trying to recruit. During 1990 it created new trainee programmes, based around its brands, which give young graduates the opportunity to work abroad. The programmes last two years and aim to give young trainee managers both a thorough grounding in the business brand and an international orientation.

These programmes will be run by the brands themselves. The only stipulation from the corporate centre is that the brands should try to recruit half of their trainees from outside France, and that half of the group should be women. The latter request stems from Accor's strong awareness of changing demographic trends in Europe and the predicted decline in the numbers of young men during the 1990s.

Graduates on the two-year programme receive training in brand management in their home country for a year. They then go abroad for a year to work at several sites where they can acquire practical experience of working in a hotel and gain an insight into different national markets. On return the young managers may be promoted to general manager or they can gain experience in a larger hotel.

Hoechst's international industrial scholarships

As part of a new approach to international recruitment, Hoechst UK sent five of its young recruits in 1989 on an industrial scholarship scheme run by its parent group in Germany. The pilot scheme was partly motivated by a shortage of candidates for the German training scheme as a result of adverse demographic trends.[6] It also fell into the context of a review that Hoechst carried out of the type of people it will need to employ once it has restructured its organisation into three main global business areas – the Far East, the Americas and Europe.

It was recognised that this new style would need new managers. Ian Peacock, head of personnel at Hoechst UK, describes these as:

> "General managers of broad background and expertise, able to operate in business units functioning across Europe and not limited to individual countries. Although English is likely to be the business language, local language knowledge is still needed to understand people and their culture, as well as to establish important business relationships."

The course, which Peacock likens to a mini-MBA, lasts two-and-a-half years and leads to a diploma which, it is hoped, will gain full recognition across Europe after 1992. It is in three main parts:

1. Practical training during which the apprentices are expected to hold down a job in personnel, purchasing, marketing and production. All trainees are expected to spend time working on the shopfloor to gain real experience of production.
2. Formal training at the *Berufsschule*, a school funded by local government, where subjects such as law and accountancy are covered.
3. Internal training, where word processing, computing and languages are taught at Hoechst AG's own training centre.

The five pioneering British apprentices were reported as "very successful ambassadors for the Hoechst UK scheme and for British youth. They have impressed the Hoechst managers involved with them in Frankfurt, and they have integrated well with the young Germans with whom they work." Indeed, the pilot scheme has been so successful that Hoechst AG is now considering re-aligning its whole training function on a European or international basis.

Fiat's international search for talent

Like Olivetti, Fiat is increasing its efforts to attract young talent from abroad and to find better ways of integrating it into the company. In addition to sending young Italian recruits abroad for an "employee orientation" period, it is bringing more young recruits from abroad to Italy for training courses.

Fiat believes that the process of integration must start early.

> "Transplanting such a strong culture is very difficult in any case. It is even more difficult when you add a new company culture and a new national culture. If you want to have good Fiat managers in France or the UK, when you employ young people, you must make the values of the company explicit right from the beginning so they can understand you."

Fiat expected some difficulties in encouraging young people of other nationalities to come to Italy but has been surprised by their keenness. It has found that young women are now more inclined to go abroad and is also making greater efforts to attract more of them.

The qualities to look for

What qualities should international companies look for when recruiting young people? Some companies certainly feel that evidence of international travel or linguistic ability are useful indicators of potential internationalism. Others believe, however, that there is still plenty of time to instil an international outlook. What is more important as a starting-point is breadth of outlook – people, who, as Unilever puts it, have shown the desire and curiosity to cross boundaries and to move from the security of what they know.

Unilever has long believed in recruiting high-quality talent and providing career development that is useful for both the company and the recruit. Quality of recruitment continues to be a basic concern and the company invests a great deal of time and effort in it. Unilever is said to have been the first company in the UK to have sent recruiters into the universities in the "milk round" to identify and hire promising graduates. The Unilever recruiting process is reportedly one of the stiffest tests that any new graduate can face.

Once recruited, new arrivals at Unilever are given some "hands-on" experience and responsibility for achieving results to confirm their potential. Increasingly, this early career experience is involving issues which cross national and cultural boundaries. This does not necessarily mean working abroad, but that they should somehow be exposed to what Tony Vineall, Unilever's deputy director of personnel, calls the "messiness" that arises when trying to carry out a cross-border task. It also involves, where possible, working in a team that includes different nationalities. Providing this sort of experience is becoming easier to arrange because Unilever's businesses have been reorganised transnationally so that, for example, people in a European powders marketing group will have their boss in London, and people in a bar soap group will have their ultimate boss in Hamburg.

In the experience of TSB's Stanic, fluency in the English language is becoming an increasingly important factor in pan-European graduate recruitment.[7] He notes that some British companies:

> "... are now actively recruiting in the more anglophone continental universities, particularly in the European North-West. Many professional bodies or firms encompassing the accountancy, medical and legal professions are finding it worthwhile to recruit at considerable distances in English-speaking countries of the old Commonwealth, with good results."

He notes a reciprocal trend for organisations based on the continent of Europe, particularly in service industries, to require young trainees and apprentices to spend some time speaking English and working in the UK. British trainees, with a legacy of limited and inadequate language teaching in their schools, might not be expected to be the internationalists most sought after by foreign companies. However, recent statistics have indicated that 15,000 Britons take up jobs on the continent annually compared with only 5,000 who return, while 2 million Britons are estimated to be working outside the UK of which an increasingly significant proportion are employed in Europe.[8]

Recruiting senior managers

It is not only the market for graduates that is becoming international. More and more firms with international ambitions are seeking senior managers with international experience. David Kay, chairman of search consultants Goddard Kay Rogers & Associates, believes that companies gain positive benefits from recruiting senior managers from outside. "However capable they are at developing their own people, any organisation must benefit from time to time from filling jobs at senior level from outside and from bringing in new ideas."

He warns, however, that the single European market will not mean that managers are automatically transferable from one country to another.

> "If a French company wants a managing director, it will be a very bold person who puts in a German rather than a French person to run that company. It is a question of relationships and people sometimes forget about the differences in culture! These differences will remain for a very long time and to ignore them is very dangerous. On the other hand, moving within a company is different because you know the culture of the company. The French would know the German had been a very successful manager and would know him or her as a colleague."

A study by another firm of search consultants, Saxton Bampfylde, confirms that managers who can operate across national frontiers are in short supply in Europe.[9] It suggests that the *ideal* "Euro-executive" comes from a small European country – for example, the Dutch and Scandinavians "have always had to seek their fortunes elsewhere", and tend to have early experience of adaptation and survival in two or more cultures and/or languages, perhaps at school or university. The ideal Euro-executive, it maintains, has a real interest in new cultures and markets, proven organisational adaptability, speaks other languages with true fluency especially during international negotiations, has line experience in another culture, and has had experience of a major multinational. The stock of this commodity is small; "but the small group that does exist will be the target of intense competition, not only throughout Europe but from businesses outside the Community which are anxious to enter the European market."

If there are still relatively few cross-border operators, John Viney, managing partner of search consultants Heidrick & Struggles, believes that their numbers are growing. Very few of the pre-second world war generation are international and most are rooted in one country. The post-war generation, on the other hand, has many more people who have had significant international exposure. More are of mixed parentage and have been exposed to more than one culture from an early age. Many more have spent their holidays with families in other countries, and some will even have gone to foreign business schools.

The new generation of young Europeans are different again. They have a common code of dress, listen to the same music, share similar values, and mix together easily. This generation, says Viney, will produce more and more people who can cross the boundaries.

Recruiting senior managers from outside can also have its difficulties, as Unilever has recognised. While it has traditionally filled most of its senior posts from its own pool of managers, it expects the recruitment market for graduates and other categories of people to be very competitive for the rest of the decade. The company is now making provision for more mid-career recruits. It is aware that such managers will have problems entering the strong web of informal relationships which longer-serving managers have built up and on which the company depends. Unilever therefore has planned for their integration into the network of informal relationships. Mid-career recruits are provided with mentors as well as an introductory three-day seminar on "Understanding How Unilever Operates".

Some do's and don'ts

The complexities of international recruitment have been well illustrated by Keith Allen, an academic researcher who used to be vice-president, human resources policies, for Northern Telecom World

Trade in Toronto.[10] Allen cites the example of a British company that was seeking a plant manager for an engineering subsidiary in Holland. Believing that local operations should be run by local people, it wanted to recruit a Dutch national. This immediately raised a host of questions for the British company's personnel director. Where should he advertise? What language should be used for the advertisement? Should he use the company's standard application form? What were the customs relating to invitation to interview – during the day or in the evening? What language would be best for the interviews (the personnel director spoke no Dutch)? What was an appropriate salary level? What were the customs relating to continuity of fringe benefits? What kind of contract was usual?

After much deliberation the company decided to advertise in Dutch in the local engineering professional journals; to use a Dutch application form or ask candidates to present their own style of CV; and to interview in Dutch. The successful candidate was someone who had been a plant manager for five years in a similar company and who wanted to run a larger factory. But the personnel director did not immediately rejoice at finding such an apparently ideal candidate to fill the post, for he had recently read a survey which revealed that three out of five local nationals working for foreign employers are rated unsatisfactory after three years in the job.

Keith Allen advocates the following rules for recruiting local nationals.

- Rigorously assess the skills that are essential to do the job.
- Do not manufacture unnecessary restrictions not required by local firms and which will therefore exclude good candidates (language, corporate forms and procedures that are unusual in the country in question).
- Ask advice; in all countries the information needed is usually available.
- Do not assume anything is the same as in the home country simply because it seems like it. Always check.
- Check the candidate's understanding by asking the same question several times in different ways. The worst kind of misunderstanding is when everyone is sure they understood.

When using an executive search consultancy, Allen recommends:

- Avoid surprises by developing a team-type working relationship with your consultant.
- Do not always go to the search agencies you know. Check each assignment requirement against track record.
- Take an interest in the personal as well as the professional background of international candidates; things which are private when working in one country can sometimes produce great difficulties – nationality of wife and children, adopted children, tax status, membership of national or "special deal" benefit plans. The list can be long, varied and full of surprises.

Recruiting international directors

At the top end of the recruitment spectrum, as we saw in Chapter 3, some companies are creating multicultural boards by recruiting directors (often non-executive) from the countries in which they operate. This is likely to become more common. Travel costs may increase and some communications problems can arise (boards are likely to make increasing use of communications technology including international conference calling and video-conferencing). But by bringing a different perspective, plus in-depth knowledge of their own countries and regions, such directors have a potentially powerful contribution to make to the company's international strategy-making.

It might be suggested that internationalisation should indeed start at the top of the company and that the recruitment of overseas directors is one of the first steps that a company bent on internationalisation should consider. John Viney, who specialises in helping companies to recruit non-executive directors from other countries, however warns against the temptation to recruit a "token" foreigner.

Recruiting such directors is a complex process. On the one hand, there are problems of integrating people from different countries into an effective team. Corporate boards function differently in other countries and fiduciary requirements differ significantly from country to country. What is expected of a non-executive director will also vary between countries; in some they may not be expected to do very much. This raises questions of how the non-executive director's job is to be defined and how performance is to be measured. It is not enough simply to appoint one or more people from other countries on to the board, however talented they may appear on paper.

Where appointments are handled carefully, a multicultural board may be very effective. John Viney describes one particularly interesting innovation where a company that was going global set up a global advisory board for the chief executive. This consists of six chief executives from around the world, including the USA and the Pacific Rim. These CEOs are themselves from companies with an interest in global issues and are people who enjoy the challenge and want to learn from others. "They want to learn new tricks and ways of doing things, and also ways of not doing things."

Possibly these chief executives exemplify the very quality that is most important to look for when recruiting the international managers of the future – that capacity for life-long learning described in Chapter 3.

References

1 V. Stanic,"Recruiting in an international market place", *The Personnel Manager's Yearbook 1990*, pp. 21-28.
2 C. Hogg and M. Syrett,"Getting the right management for 1992", *Director,* March 1989, pp. 101-103.
3 R. Pearson, "Hunt for Euro-talent won't be all one way", *Sunday Times,* Section E, May 28, 1989.
4 Incomes Data Services, *Recruitment,* Institute of Personnel Management European Management Guide, 1990.
5 V. Stanic, *op. cit.*
6 I. Peacock, "The Hoechst industrial scholarship scheme", *Executive Development*, vol. 3, no. 4, 1990, pp. 3-6.
7 V. Stanic, *op. cit.*
8 V. Stanic, *op. cit.*
9 Saxton Bampfylde International PLC, *The Search for the Euro-Executive,* June 1989.
10 K. Allen, "Making the right choices in international recruitment", *Personnel Management,* October 1989, pp. 56-59.

CHAPTER 7

EDUCATING INTERNATIONAL MANAGERS

Some companies have long believed that the experience of their managers should be supplemented by education, and in many firms management education is coming to play a wider and more strategic part. In this chapter, we examine how management education can assume a crucial and central role in shaping the international company.

Creating a common culture

In-company management programmes help to create the mutual understanding and the informal networks which have been identified as crucial to a corporate international spirit. Indeed, companies such as Electrolux view the creation of a common corporate culture as almost a higher priority for their international management programmes than the development of individual skills. General Electric, which puts great effort into management education, starts the process very early by bringing graduate recruits from around the world to its training centre within six months of joining the firm so that they begin to understand the company culture and start to form links across the organisation.

International management development programmes are seen increasingly as vehicles for managers to work on strategic issues. We see a significant change taking place whereby *management training* centres are effectively becoming *strategy development* centres. They are becoming agents of change, as at General Electric, for example, where international action learning by teams of managers is translated into organisational learning (described later in this chapter).

In firms such as GE and Unilever, planned experience is supplemented by a core sequence of management programmes which are timed to coincide with transition points in people's careers. It is significant that these companies give much more emphasis to internationalising the whole of the curriculum than to setting up special courses on "international management" which they see as encouraging a view that international management is something separate from normal business. By the time someone reaches senior management in Unilever, he or she will have probably attended four or five programmes in each of which they have worked with four or five different sets of people drawn from 20 nationalities. This experience changes in a very positive manner the way that people think about other nationalities and cultures.

Not all multinational companies take this view. Shell, which like Unilever, has a deeply embedded dual nationality, tackles intercultural training overtly by including it in its career development programme. Sue Davison, who runs a consultancy specialising in cross-cultural audits, suggests that Shell's Inter-Cultural Communication Workshop for new graduate recruits is "probably unique".[1] This is a one-week residential course on the seven-month graduate induction programme run both in the UK and the Netherlands. The stated objective of the course is to "understand what is meant by a culture and its influence on an individual's values, and to increase cultural awareness". At senior levels Shell runs specific programmes on negotiating across cultures, identifying corporate culture, and managing multicultural teams. "Participants not only consider national differences but also interdepartmental cultural differences and 'emerging' cultures such as the green culture in Scandinavia. The emphasis is on creating an awareness of the issues, and not on giving a prescriptive recipe for dealing with them."

Unilever courses

In contrast, Unilever prefers to take a more low-key approach to international training. It believes that a programme of central courses focused on the needs of managers at set career stages can provide focal points for the evolution of the international corporate culture as well as the development of individuals. Initial training takes place within the national company, where programmes differ according to local educational systems. But by the time that employees have any type of management job (about 3–4 years after joining the company), the training becomes almost totally international.

In addition to ensuring that courses bring together participants from all parts of the organisation and that the content has an appropriate focus, Unilever believes that it is imperative to have a wide range of different nationalities among the teaching faculty. Their different views also illuminate the business issues involved in different international markets.

The first training programme at Unilever to coincide with a major career transition point is the International Management Seminar for people in their mid- to late-20s. This is when they first become responsible for significant numbers of people or resources or, where specialists are concerned, when they start to make a significant contribution. The main emphasis here is on managing people. The second programme is the General Managers' Course for people about to become operating company directors. At the third stage, after they have "graduated" from Unilever's own general management course, senior managers are generally sent on external programmes at business schools. The fourth level is the Senior Strategy Programme for senior managers.

It is policy at Unilever to move people around within the programme so they come into contact with as many nationalities as possible. In a two-week programme, for example, participants can expect to be in three or four different syndicate groups and to work with a dozen different nationalities.

The Electrolux programmes

Training and education have also evolved at Electrolux into something far more than the improvement of expertise. In the past, the company has relied on finding new management talent through acquisitions. It has now become much more concerned to build and educate its own cadre of internationalists and is giving more attention to international management education. Its formal programmes have three main aims:

- To develop managerial excellence because product quality starts with management quality.

- To do without bureaucracy, using the programmes as a forum where people will meet, learn and understand each other and create informal networks.
- To encourage corporate development through meetings of top management to talk about their vision and strategies and at the same time "be questioned by the people who will be running the Electrolux of tomorrow and who are closer to the feelings of the world".

Ultimately, therefore, the Electrolux programmes are about implementing global strategies and about giving a sense of ownership to those who have to implement them.

The content of the programmes is directly related to the strategy of the company and its units. Although they include state-of-the-art input from leading business academics and coaching by top management, they are seen as forums for practical and relevant debate rather than as traditional "courses". They are also intended to be heavily results-oriented. Just as the company's strategy and structure are in evolution, however, so too are these programmes continuously revised and modified to reflect changing business needs.

The Electrolux International Executive Programme, introduced in 1988, is held once a year for selected high-potential managers aged 33–43, who are already in senior jobs involving international responsibilities, usually at the level of general manager of a country business. It consists of three modules held at intervals, each in a different country such as Sweden, Switzerland or the USA, and lasts in total about 4–5 weeks. The first module considers the Electrolux context for management, cultural integration, environmental analysis and strategic management. The second module looks at functional strategies, business alliances, international organisation and management, and includes a business game. The third module covers media management and leadership. Throughout the programme each participant works on a project of strategic significance for their own business. Participants, many of whom will not have met each other before, are drawn from four or five countries.

Overall the programme is seen as aiding corporate development, generating synergy and energy, rather than as an educational exercise. Faculty are drawn from top management and leading business academics and the content of the programme includes "success stories" from Electrolux and other companies. Among its aims are the development of a common corporate identity and culture, an international perspective and the creation of international networks. Electrolux believes that a common identity is emerging already. "Country identity means less and less," says Kurt Vikersjö, Electrolux's executive development manager, "and more and more we see the capabilities of people instead of their nationalities." The company also believes that international networks are starting to develop as people increasingly call each other to share problems, seek expertise or do business.

The Electrolux International Business Leadership Programme, a recent initiative, has been established in conjunction with Ashridge Management College in the UK. It is for managers in their late 20s who hold a senior position in the general management team of a business and who are required to contribute to cross-border management decisions, either in resourcing or in marketing and selling. The aims include supporting and speeding up the transition from a functional to a general management focus within a multinational setting, stimulating entrepreneurial flair across national boundaries, understanding globalisation issues affecting the participants' businesses and experience of working in English as the company language. Once again, networking is regarded as a major objective of the programme.

Electrolux is concerned to identify potential for international management early on. "The younger we identify people, the easier it is to make them international." In Sweden the company is piloting a programme to introduce younger people to the job of management, to give them opportunities for self-assessment and to assess their potential. This includes an assessment of their inter-cultural sensitivity, carried out by watching their behaviour in group tasks.

Fiat's travelling seminars

As a result of its "internationalisation of management" project, Fiat has revised its management education and training programmes to give both content and methods a greater international focus. In conjunction with ISVOR-Fiat, the company's management training centre, both the management course for future group directors (*Corso Formazione Direzionale* – CFD) and the Fiat management course for company managers (*Corso Fiat per la Gestione* – CFG) have been given a greater international slant, with particular emphasis on the international business contexts of the Fiat companies. More speakers and teachers on the programmes now come from abroad and the case studies used are Fiat cases set in an international context.

One week of the four-week CFD programme is spent abroad, including visits to local Fiat head offices. The CFG has widened the study of the Fiat business world from an Italian context to a European one, dedicating two days of the 20-day residential course to a study of Europe – the region that Fiat now regards as its domestic market. In 1989 the CFG was renamed the International Fiat Management Course.

Fiat has also introduced "travelling seminars" aimed at its top 350 managers. Teams of about 15 spend a week in the USA, Japan and other European countries visiting leading world-class companies (sometimes including competing car firms) to learn about their approaches to strategic issues such as quality, customer service, and strategic alliances. On their return, the teams' findings are fed into the company through debriefings, meetings and written reports. One particularly important result so far is that Fiat is now treating quality management as a strategic issue and is introducing a total quality programme.

Despite their brevity, Fiat is convinced that these seminars have a powerful impact in changing managers' attitudes. "Our people are still rooted in their culture," says Vittorio Tesio, vice-president for management development and planning. As a result of the seminars, "our managers can see the world is different, and they also see our competitors are doing very good things, and that if we don't update and change our behaviour, we are going to have problems".

Fiat has also taken advantage of an exchange agreement between the EC and Japan to send a few managers to Japan. A group of personnel specialists spent three weeks in Japan, for example, studying Japanese approaches to human resource management.

The "Fiat Italian Briefing" is a programme which is designed for non-Italian managers of Fiat companies throughout the world. In addition to helping managers build up a more thorough command of the Italian language, it provides a framework to help them interpret Italy and the Fiat world. Although conceived as a training programme, the course has had wider benefits in terms of integrating people from countries into the spirit and culture of the company.

In addition, Fiat has introduced "Country Briefings" (*Briefing Paese*), seminars held in the country concerned for managers from the various companies within the group who operate in international markets. The seminars are designed to enable the manager to understand the most salient features of another culture. In particular, they try to change the stereotypes that Italians have of different countries. Managers are thus helped to find the best ways to relate to, and integrate successfully into, different business contexts.

In the area of communications and foreign languages, Fiat has devised another programme called Presentation Techniques to develop language skills and the use of more appropriate communication models for an international audience. It aims to help individuals express themselves publicly in English through the use of verbal and non-verbal techniques.

Fiat believes that it is very important to start the internationalisation process at an early age. It runs an English-language programme for its young graduates which involves an intensive course of 100 hours integrated into their introductory five-month training programme. The aim of the programme is not only to equip future executives with an "indispensable work tool", but also to give new recruits a strong signal that they will be working in an international environment and that they need to look beyond the narrow Italian context. Language teaching for Fiat has a wider meaning than language learning *per se*. The important thing to realise, says Tesio, is that an emphasis on inter-cultural competence "shifts the focus from teaching languages to teaching people to understand other cultures".

The emphasis in the language course is also on speaking "English as an international language". Fiat does not intend for the moment to make English the company language. "Since 85 per cent of our managers communicate in Italian, we think that the other 15 per cent should be able to communicate in Italian within the company."

Global action learning at GE

GE's Management Development Institute at Crotonville, near New York, is playing a central role in the radical transformation of the company culture and in developing the global skills required by the corporation. As Rosabeth Moss Kanter says, it is "much more than a corporate college; it is in effect a synergy centre that helps people identify shared interests across businesses and tackle common problems together".[2]

In becoming an instrument of change and synergy, Crotonville itself has undergone significant changes in its approach to management education. Under the leadership of Dr James Baughman, GE's manager of corporate management development, the curriculum has been transformed from a focus on developing individual skills to one that also helps to bring about fundamental organisational change.

This has involved, in some of the more advanced management development programmes, a move away from classroom teaching. While classroom teaching is still highly effective for some knowledge-based areas, Crotonville has now introduced a "higher impact, behavioural" workshop approach based on action learning in teams where people bring actual work problems with them, rather than focus on historical case studies which may not relate to their particular experience.

The advantages of action learning include the fact that people learn more effectively by doing; that they have to learn to work in teams; and that the learning takes place in "real time", involving real and substantive issues requiring decisions. It also puts participants in the role of problem-solver. As James Noel, programme manager at Crotonville, says: "The amount of learning transferred back to the participant's work setting is likely to be higher and the company can capture the considerable brain power invested in solving some of its real issues."[3] In the action learning approach, participants wrestle with very difficult, unresolved, emotionally charged real business problems, rather than case studies. They argue among themselves, and work through intense team-building experiences. The measure of success of a programme shifts from their evaluation of how good they felt about the learning experience to how the experience influences their organisation and their leadership behaviour over time.

In recognition of GE's increasing internationalisation, Crotonville has abandoned a two-week international management course which it set up in the early 1980s. It did not feel that this course addressed the real challenge of global issues which it now wants to weave into the full range of management education. It also believes that thinking globally requires more than knowledge; people must actually learn how to manage in the more complex and fast-moving global environment.

Moments of opportunity

GE believes that over 80 per cent of such learning and development takes place through the job and that the other 20 per cent comes from formal development activities. It is therefore important to identify the most appropriate points in their careers when individuals should take part in a development programme. GE's "core development sequence" is based on five development stages and four transition points called "moments of opportunity" or "teachable moments" at which Crotonville intervenes to provide a formal development experience. The programme has been given considerable thought and is comprehensive. We feel that it is worth examining in some detail as an example of an organisation that has sought to make management education a prime force in organisational change, strategy implementation and global learning.

Throughout the GE management development sequence three interdependent themes are addressed in ways appropriate to each level (see Figure 7.1 on page 147). The themes are based on the three prime qualities that GE tries to encourage in its managers – "global brains" (or "global maturity and sophistication"), technical and business "best practices", and leadership abilities (outlined in Chapter 4). A major objective of all the programmes that follow is to establish networks between people from the earliest moment; "people that you can call upon, who are sufficiently in the same game as you." The second objective is to establish "certain standards of play and behaviour so that GE people in Taiwan, India or Brazil are playing to the same standards and employing the same rules".

The GE management development sequence starts with the Corporate Entry Leadership Conference where GE's newly hired

Figure 7.1 **The three independent themes of GE management development**

	Developing "global" maturity and sophistication	Developing technical and business best practices	Developing leadership abilities
For business leaders			
For functional leaders			
For experienced managers			
For new managers			
For individual contributors			
At entry level			

Source: General Electric

graduates are brought to Crotonville to learn about GE's global strategy and competitors and about the changing GE values. The second stage of the sequence begins with the one-week New Manager Development Programme which is attended by all managers newly appointed to manage other professionals within a year of their appointment. The programme aims to help people make the transition from being an individual contributor to leading others and creating high-performing teams. This programme is now offered around the world and is tailored to four different regions: the USA, Asia–Pacific, Europe and Latin America. It takes into account such differences as the more community-centred approach of the Japanese and the more conservative approach of the Latin Americans to the role of women. The company also finds that different approaches towards ethical standards, environmental issues, employment practices and to what constitutes a fair day's work have to be considered.

The second stage also includes the Experienced Manager Programme for people with substantial experience irrespective of current potential for advancement. It aims to "empower GE managers as developers, leaders and agents of change". This programme is run around the world and is action learning oriented in its approach. Baughman describes this course as "a masterclass"; people can bring a problem that they are currently working on to the class and benefit from working on it as a group.

Stage three of the sequence comprises advanced courses for people in a strategic position in their function such as marketing, finance, manufacturing or human resources. These mostly take place at Crotonville and bring together top functional specialists from around the world. In these largely classroom-based programmes, lasting several weeks, people are exposed to state-of-the-art thinking in their respective functions with the aim of ensuring that they are operating at the leading edge. They also work on change projects and may invite senior line managers such as their bosses or major clients to Crotonville for several days to work on the projects too.

These programmes are becoming "multi-functional" and each class aims to include 25–30 per cent of participants from outside the function in question. The content has also evolved considerably under the impact of globalisation. The advent of satellite communications, for example, has meant that greater attention is given to information technology. In finance there is much more emphasis on exchange and commodity management. (GE purchases huge amounts of commodities such as copper and tungsten internationally.) The human resource area is much more concerned with cultural diversity.

The functional programme with the most international flavour is the Impact Programme which focuses on global best practice in the manufacturing and engineering area. With the aim of making significant improvements in their own businesses, participants examine the current practices of world manufacturers from the point of view of quality, workforce management, materials management and technology. After a week of classroom exposure to state-of-the-art ideas, they spend a week in Asia on in-depth visits to Japanese and South Korean establishments such as Fanuc, Toshiba, Daewoo and

Samsung. They return to Crotonville to synthesise what they have learned before spending another week visiting European manufacturers like Thomson, Philips and Fiat.

A particularly fascinating aspect of the Impact Programme is that participants actually visit GE competitors. This was not as difficult to arrange as might have been expected. Richard Kennedy, the Crotonville education manager who created the programme, says that when he first approached Japanese companies, he told them: "The people who manage your businesses and factories will learn as much from our questions as we will from your answers."

Stage four of the management development sequence involves three executive programmes taken over a 5–8 year period, each lasting four weeks, and which all focus on global competitiveness. These consist of the Manager Development Course which considers the problems of managing a multi-mission, multi-functional organisation; the Business Management Course for potential general managers which addresses the business strategies and leadership skills needed to succeed in a competitive global environment; and the Executive Development Course for potential top managers which builds on the first two programmes and promotes an understanding of senior level leadership in the global environment.

The development sequence culminates at the fifth stage in occasional senior management workshops in which groups of 20–30 top-level executives address unresolved company-wide issues together with the chief executive.

The second programme in stage four of the sequence , the Business Management Course (BMC), is a particularly exciting programme. This is an experiential course that seeks to apply the principles of action learning to the full. It lasts a month, is run three times a year and is an entirely action learning based programme organised around consulting projects which participants carry out on behalf of various GE businesses. The aim of the programme is to help participants, who come from all over the world, to learn, apply and receive feedback on business concepts and skills applied to real GE business issues; to develop leadership and team skills; and to develop personal action plans to apply their new skills in their jobs. An equally important objective is to provide help on important issues to GE businesses.

After two weeks of immersion in state-of-the-art management concepts, ranging from strategic marketing to competitive analysis and organisational change, participants are divided into six teams, each of five or six members, to focus on the business projects. There are three projects, each of which is proposed by a GE business and sponsored by the head of that business. Two teams work independently on each project, thus providing the business with two sets of recommendations and also introducing an element of competition. The team travels to the relevant business where it has access to all key managers, including the head of the business, and all business data. The team is also free to talk to customers and competitors. The teams return to Crotonville to report their findings and recommendations to top managers from the businesses concerned. "Very quickly, participants find themselves in a tough, open exchange defending their recommendations."

Examples of BMC action learning projects have included evaluation of options for the major appliances business, analyses of opportunities for the use of artificial intelligence in different GE businesses, and recommendations on a joint venture partner to the construction equipment business. The businesses receive a piece of consultancy which may have direct financial benefit, such as the team which identified potential additional sales of $200 million a year for its sponsoring business. "The acid test of success," says Noel, "is that the businesses keep coming back for more."

The course has been given an increasingly global dimension. Since 1988 one of the three annual BMCs has been held at INSEAD, the European business school at Fontainebleau near Paris. The aim of the course is to provide the participants, who are mostly Americans, with a European perspective on business skills such as marketing, business alliances, working in a cross-cultural environment, and on the European political and economic scene. GE considers that this cultural exposure is a very valuable aspect of the overseas experiences, and it therefore choses locations that offer total cultural immersion. "Our people live in town, mix with the locals, have to find their own meals and newspapers, and figure out how to mail a letter and make a phone call, so it's a real experience on a round-the-clock basis for the participants."

Best practices visits
In addition to the huge effort that GE puts into its core development sequence, one other activity provides international learning both for individual managers and for the organisation as a whole. In 1989, GE initiated a study of best practices in productivity. A dozen high-productivity companies were selected from industries in the USA and Japan to which GE can relate. A team of consultants and "hard-nosed" line managers spent time in the companies to find out how they achieve higher productivity. Their report became the basis for study and debate throughout the whole company. GE has held seminars, workshops and team discussions to "blow" the findings through the company and to challenge the company's current performance.

GE does not talk about itself as a learning organisation but this is precisely what it is trying to be – on a global scale. It wants its managers wherever they are to open their eyes to the world from the moment they join the company. It wants to learn from best practice wherever it might be found, whether this resides in competitors or other companies, and to turn this into organisational change. Clearly, GE's international efforts in global education, particularly its action learning techniques, demand considerable investment and commitment. It believes, however, that compared with the cost-effectiveness of traditional development programmes, the action learning approach provides excellent value.

Universities without walls

Like GE, many of the companies that see education at the core of their internationalisation programmes maintain substantial central management training centres. The location of the "academy" of French hotel and restaurant group Accor, situated alongside the company's head office at Evry, signifies its strong commitment to training and development. With 100 bedrooms and about 30 trainers from the USA, the UK, France, Germany and Belgium, it is a substantial symbol of collective learning. There are plans to establish a "satellite academy" in Brazil.

While such centres are the focal point of many companies' training courses, a number of firms, like Johnson & Johnson and Pepsi-Cola International, are seeking to increase the international impact of education by taking corporate training programmes to overseas locations, wherever in the world is most appropriate. J&J calls this approach "universities without walls". The newly created Pepsi-Cola International Management Institute, for example, aims to take management training to its franchise bottlers around the world.

Ericsson set up the Ericsson Management Institute in 1989 to support the company's new worldwide management planning process. This is not a centrally located training centre; it consists of a number of carefully considered core management courses (some of which are still being developed) which bring together Ericsson managers from all over the world and which can be held wherever is most appropriate.

The importance that Ericsson attributes to management development and education is reflected in the composition of the institute's steering group. It consists of the company's chief executive, the managing director of the telecommunications business area (Ericsson's biggest business), the managing director of the cables and network business area, the corporate marketing director and the senior vice-president for human resources. The steering group's role is to approve nominations, suggest strategic issues for project work, approve course designs, structures and budgets, and to evaluate programmes.

The Ericsson Senior Executive Programme (ESEP) has been created to cater for the top 300 managers in the group. It involves about 25 participants at a time and lasts three weeks, the first two of which are held outside Sweden. The aim of the first module is to help managers develop analytical and strategic concepts and to provide them with some instruments and methods for considering the business and its strategy. The managers work on strategically important subjects such as a real case study involving the in-depth analysis of a particular market.

The institute is not expected to employ large numbers of people and currently it has only one full-time and two part-time programme directors. The company brings in outside experts from educational institutes or business schools, but the programmes are not like traditional business school courses. The intention is not to shower participants with academic concepts. "These are senior, experienced people who are managing directors of companies, so you cannot just sit them on a chair and teach at them." The programmes are designed to be very interactive and people must see the use of them in their own businesses. This is reinforced by the fact that the businesses themselves pay a fee for sending people on the programmes.

The second part of the ESEP lasts one week and takes place in Sweden. This consists of a "strategic dialogue" where the participants meet the chief executive and the company's top managers to debate company ambitions and strategy. Thus the programme becomes part of the process of developing Ericsson's strategies.

The Ericsson Management Programme (EMP) has a target group of 1,500 middle managers from around the world. It is held twice a year, lasts five weeks and covers such areas as finance, marketing and human resource management, which will be integrated through the use of business games.

In addition to the ESEP and EMP programmes, Ericsson is also introducing a series of functional programmes, of which the first three will be Human Resource Management, International Marketing and Project Management. The company is also developing leadership programmes for junior and middle managers as a basis for its worldwide management planning system. It wants to run the programmes on "a global basis", providing a common framework that brings together the different approaches that all the Ericsson businesses have developed in this area.

The role of business schools

Some companies firmly believe in the importance of sending managers on business school programmes for the "outside" view that they offer. At Unilever, for instance, managers attend a business school general management course as a standard part of their career development.

It is clear, however, that the more fundamental role that companies are giving to management education poses considerable challenges for business schools. As one company said: "Business schools are 20 years behind where we need help. They are good on content but poor on process. We need help converting a lot of good strategic thinking into action and implementation, to make the link between strategy and action. In internationalisation, what will be important is support on process rather than content."

The criticism is not entirely fair. Nonetheless, it is clear that the schools need to build on their traditional strengths and widen their competence and the services that they can provide. Meeting this challenge will require great imagination and innovation. Some schools have sought to widen the international mix of their faculty and increase the number of participants from different countries; several have formed links with counterparts in other countries. All this is necessary but not sufficient. Business schools will have to think creatively about how they can set all learning in a global context and blend it with the process of implementing international strategy.

Some schools have been trying to adopt more innovative approaches to international management education both for students on full-time business courses and for managers in post. These often involve action learning approaches and/or internships with corporate sponsors. We have identified some outstanding examples.

- At the American Graduate School of International Management, better known as Thunderbird, in Glendale, Arizona, each student on the MIM (Master's of International Management) course spends 12–18 months focusing on three areas: business training in such areas as finance, accounting and marketing; proficiency in a foreign language (the school offers nine languages); and the international studies core curriculum. Here, each student focuses on studying one country in depth, including its culture, legal system and history. Thunderbird emphasises the human factors critical to international success: learning the advantages of your product in terms that the foreign market will understand, and knowing how the competition is likely to react through an understanding of the mind-set and economy of the country.
- The International Management Internship Program at Babson College in Massachusetts sends selected MBA candidates abroad for 2–3 months to carry out important projects for corporate sponsors. Babson says that interns "gain an awareness of alternative business approaches to international

commerce, broaden their professional experience base, improve their language skills, and acquire global management skills". Corporate sponsors secure consultancy on urgent company issues and a greater global business perspective is stimulated among company staff with whom the interns work. Typical projects include market research and planning, organisational analysis and development, management information system analyses, and project finance and analysis.

- The five-week Global Leadership Program at the University of Michigan is sponsored by 26 companies from the USA, Japan and Europe who undertake to send senior executives as participants each year. The programme starts with a weekend at an Outward Bound school to build up team relationships amongst the 20 or so participants. Two weeks of study are followed by two weeks abroad when the group splits into three or four teams, each of which visits an important developing country such as Brazil, China or India to research the market. The teams return to Michigan to present written, oral and video reports. One of the reported benefits of the programme is the growth of cross-cultural awareness among participants. The Japanese, for example, are said to be very patient in discussion while the Americans do plenty of talking, but gradually each become aware of the others' style and modify their own behaviour.

- The European Management Programme is a joint venture between the Universitätsseminar der Wirtschaft (USW) in Köln, Germany, the Centre de Perfectionnement aux Affaires (CPA) in Paris, France, and Ashridge Management College in the UK. Its 17-day programme takes place in at least two of the three countries. Its aim is to foster the cross-fertilisation of ideas and experiences concerning strategic and operational issues facing organisations in different countries and different sectors in the new European context. It also aims to encourage senior managers to think strategically and manage more effectively in a world economy dominated by several world centres or powers. Described as "a learning experience for executives by executives", the programme considers such issues as the strengths, weaknesses and opportunities of the single European market; internationalisation strategies; creating a pan-European corporate identity; building a pan-European production strategy; European marketing strategies; and lobbying the European Commission.

- The MBA programme at Ashridge Management College in the UK is an action learning programme for experienced managers sponsored by their companies. The programme's modular structure combines residential modules at Ashridge with company-based project work. The programme takes an integrated, interdisciplinary approach emphasising the development of general managers and business leaders who are encouraged to focus on issues with a global perspective. The project addresses a live issue of strategic importance to the company and provides an opportunity to apply the knowledge and practise the skills acquired during the residential modules. Typical projects might be an investigation of the introduction of a product into an overseas market, the development and implementation of a computerised management information system, or an investigation of the impact of cultural differences on a company's international joint venture policy.
- The MBA programme at Manchester Business School in the UK includes an International Business Project whereby companies nominate a significant international opportunity for investigation by a team of students. Each team presents a detailed proposal to its client company, carries out the agreed research and provides a confidential report on the project. The projects usually involve around 1,500 hours of investigation and the company meets the direct costs of the project. Client companies include major international companies and projects range from evaluating market entry possibilities to suggesting major restructuring of the client's international strategy.
- The University of Technology in Helsinki regularly brings Finnish managers to the UK and Belgium for 4–5 week programmes designed to make participants aware of the

nature of the European Community, the state of the competition and potential business opportunities for their companies.

Clearly, some business schools are trying to apply more imaginative approaches to international business education. In view of the need for the international manager to be a life-long learner, one of the most important contributions the business schools might make is to help managers learn how to learn.

References

1 S. Davison, "Building pan-European teams", *Eurobusiness,* July 1989, pp. 28-33.
2 R. Moss Kanter, *When Giants Learn to Dance,* Simon & Schuster, London, 1989.
3 J.L. Noel and R. Charan, "Leadership development at GE's Crotonville", *Human Resource Management,* Winter 1988, vol. 27, no. 4, pp. 434-447.

CHAPTER 8

MANAGING INTERNATIONAL ASSIGNMENTS

In recent years there has been a general decline in the number of expatriates who make a career of working abroad, as the industrially emerging nations have insisted that indigenous managers should be promoted to the highest echelons of the subsidiaries of multinational companies. International companies themselves have also come to recognise the considerable merits of encouraging local managers to head up their overseas companies. But, in contrast to this trend, a growing number of international firms are sending their most promising managers on overseas assignments to broaden their horizons and to enhance their inter-cultural competence. Many companies have begun to take the view that international experience helps to develop the kind of qualities that are required of senior executives operating in a global market place. These firms see overseas assignments as part of the management development process, not just a means of channelling technical expertise from the centre.

At International Distillers and Vintners, a subsidiary of Grand Metropolitan, overseas assignments are tailor-made around the developmental needs of the individual. For example, IDV may arrange for a manager who has come from an underdeveloped market place to get as much experience as possible in sophisticated market functions so that he or she can transfer best practices to their country on their return. Other managers may simply be sent to work for a variety of brands so as to broaden their base and help them become good general managers.

"There is no universally applicable programme. Each assignment has to be tailored to suit the experience and language skills of the 'cadre' assignee. No two programmes have been the same and few people would believe the problems we had selecting a Japanese manager for essentially a high-flyer programme against all the cultural 'seniority rules' and the unacceptability of singling out any one individual for special treatment."

Although Johnson & Johnson is committed to the principle that its overseas companies should be run by locals, it is also trying to give more of its "fast track" people international assignments. Under its International Development Programme (IDP), it tries to give middle managers in overseas companies big company experience by taking them out of their jobs and moving them to the USA. "If you're in J&J Thailand and you're the person dealing with the J&J franchise there, it's helpful to work with the J&J company that sells baby products in the USA and see what it's all about." Typically, such a person would work as a product manager in the USA for 1½–5 years before returning home to a bigger job, perhaps as a product group manager. The IDP may also involve bringing some people from abroad to take up staff appointments at head office.

J&J also has an International MBA Programme whereby it recruits each year 50–60 overseas students studying on MBA programmes in the USA and sends them to work in J&J companies in their own country. Some of them will be attached to J&J in the USA for a short time first. An added bonus of J&J's two international programmes is that they appear to reduce turnover among the ranks of the company's overseas middle managers. Some 60–70 per cent of people who have been to the USA under the IDP scheme remain with the company, a proportion that is relatively high compared with rates of attrition in other companies.

Accor views international assignments, whether long or short term, as a vital means of giving people a perspective of working in a worldwide company. "Our philosophy is that we will send someone abroad if there is an unfilled vacancy; if there is a need to transfer know-how or implement a new process; or if we wish to make a special investment in someone's career development."

The group is currently making special efforts to promote international mobility further down the organisation. It has recently introduced a new approach aimed at encouraging national managers to consider how they can give international experience to more of their staff. Accor's national managers are providing feedback on the new policy, which will help to validate its benefits.

Rhône-Poulenc sees international assignments serving a dual purpose that benefits both the employee and the company. Its assignments are intended to promote learning and a cross-fertilisation of technical business expertise throughout the group, while at the same time overcoming local skills shortages. For example, a manager will be sent to another country to help a local business develop a new product. Similarly if it has been unable to recruit suitable candidates from the local or national market, human resource managers can ask the corporate centre to help by sending an expatriate manager.

Expatriates play a crucial role at Unilever. All the company's best managers are expected to work abroad at some stage in their careers – especially those of high potential. The company has found that they are the most likely to make good use of the challenge of a job abroad and they are also the easiest to relocate on return to the home base. However, the company realises that not all overseas jobs call for high-flyers and that, when appropriate, it can be good practice to appoint an older manager whose career has "plateaued". Unilever maintains that the intrinsic rewards of a challenging job abroad for such a person should not be underestimated.

When Unilever managers are assigned to an overseas posting they typically move within the same product group. If somebody changes product group they usually do so within the same country. The company believes that one major change is enough to cope with at any single time.

The BOC Group currently has around 120 employees located in 25 countries on long-term or short-term international assignments. At the moment the main traffic is in UK nationals moving to take up international assignments in the USA. There are 21 British BOC employees working in America, but there is also considerable movement between Australia and the South Pacific. There are 11 Australian employees working in the region. BOC's American international assignees are spread across seven different foreign locations, including China, Singapore and the UK.

The policy of moving international assignees around the world has evolved gradually at BOC in line with its growing international stature. In the past the main reason for assigning an employee to an overseas location was to provide expertise that was lacking in the host country. While this is still an important factor today, Ann Howland, manager of BOC's international assignments department, sees other considerations steadily gaining ground. "We have become more international in our thinking. We are moving people not only for technical expertise, but also for management development and training." She believes that international experience will become an increasingly important criterion in appointing people to top jobs with BOC. "In the past it's not been a criterion, but whether we've planned it or not, it's beginning to look that way. Quite a number of our present senior management have international experience."[1]

It is by no means safe to assume, however, that international assignments will automatically develop the required international outlook. Our research has shown us that "international experience" does not necessarily equate with "international effectiveness". One estimate, for example, suggests that one in seven European managers sent abroad do not complete their assignment and that an even higher 30–50 per cent of US managers have to return home prematurely from overseas postings.[2] The costs of expatriate failure are high for both a company and the individual manager concerned.

Selecting assignees

Selecting managers with the right perspective and level of commitment is, therefore, paramount. Some companies believe that the greatest commitment will come from those who volunteer for an overseas assignment rather than from people who have been pressurised into working abroad. The philosophy has always prevailed in BOC, for example, that employees control their own career destinies and the same approach has largely been applied to international assignments. Those who get the assignments tend to be employees who have made up their own minds that they would like to work abroad for a period of time rather than waited to be tapped on the shoulder and invited to do so.

Until now international assignments at Accor have been organised spasmodically on an individual basis, but the company is now anxious to ensure that international career planning works in a less fragmented way. Accor staff are actively encouraged to apply for overseas assignments, which can last a matter of months or years. They have access to an internal database which tells them about opportunities within Accor. A corporate brochure describes how staff can use the system, and every two weeks an "Opportunity Flash" listing positions available within the group is distributed to employees: "Hotel Mercure Nice seeks hotel manager ... Midi-Pyrenees needs food and beverages manager." French employees can even consult this in-house "job market" on-line 24 hours a day via Minitel videotext. Any staff member may apply for the job directly. The system also includes a demand programme whereby people who are seeking advancement or transfer can either log in their resumés and job aspirations on the centralised network or forward them directly to the unit concerned.

A public and centralised system of overseas transfers can be an effective way of combatting a danger endemic in all companies – the fact that some line managers can be understandably reluctant to lose some of their brightest people. International Distillers & Vintners is aware of this potential problem. Its tactic is for senior managers to try to ensure that the "losing" manager is acknowledged for putting the company as a whole before his or her business or department. In general, IDV has not experienced any lack of co-operation on the part of its line managers. Often these are the very people who have recognised the potential of the assignee in the first place.

As it became an increasingly global business, Johnson & Johnson experienced the opposite problem. It found a certain reluctance among its managers to take up jobs abroad, as Win Holzman explains: "If you hire very competitive people, the last thing they want is to be put into what they consider a backwater country and to then have to come back to the USA. They do not see that as part of a significant development pattern."

The company is now introducing what Holzman calls a "reverse IDP" to send younger, middle managers from head office to assignments in the company's overseas subsidiaries. For example, a young manager from Janssen, an important J&J subsidiary in Belgium, recently moved to head office in the USA, while a manager from the central compensation department went to the Belgian subsidiary, to spend a year "helping them with some of their problems and concerns in this area".

In contrast, BOC's approach to international assignments is much less structured. In general, the company expects its employees to take the intitiative. For example, employees may voice their interest in working abroad during a performance appraisal; similarly, someone might spot an announcement on the company notice board that BOC has acquired a new company abroad or entered into a new joint venture with an overseas partner, and accordingly ask about any possible overseas assignments.

> "When we first advertised the job of general manager in China we were surprised by the number and calibre of people who applied, because we couldn't see necessarily where it fitted into their career pattern or what is was going to do for them in career terms. In some instances, it was simply that it was China and they wanted that experience."

But while BOC encourages self-selection, it still takes care to ensure that those who do get an overseas posting are up to the mark.

> "International assignments are a very expensive way of sending people anywhere. It's probably three times as expensive as keeping them at home. When you're talking about sending someone from the US to the UK, it's probably five times more expensive than employing a local national. Because of this, our people have to demonstrate by performance and depth of BOC experience that they are the right people to go."

IDV believes it is important that both the placement company and the assignee manager have a shared understanding of the aims of the assignment.

> "We need to ensure that the assignee manager understands that he or she is there to do a specific job and not solely for personal development. However, we also need to stress to national managers that

assignees might require additional attention or time off for training. In other words, there has to be a trade-off between the longer-term nature of the assignment and the immediate job requirements. In most cases we persuade the local managers that these trade-offs are worthwhile because they are getting a high-calibre individual."

Ericsson, which is aiming to move more of its employees between different countries as a key element of its management planning programme, believes that it is all too often tempting to select managers from the corporate network rather than spending a little more time and effort looking for them in the subsidiary groups. The company's new worldwide management planning system is designed to avoid this shortcoming. The company also hopes that it will be able to provide people with international experience *before* they take up management posts. "We have to try to make this exchange more frequent than in the past. When we find these talented people, it is important to let them go abroad very early so they can have international experience before they go into management."

Companies with categorisation systems
Rhône-Poulenc takes a lot of trouble to match its international assignees to the specific jobs available in overseas locations. It achieves this through a job categorisation system which the company has had in place for many years. The system has eight levels, with Rhône-Poulenc's president and executive directors on level one and a newly appointed junior manager at level eight. Each categorisation specifically lists the tasks, responsibilities, necessary skills and degree of complexity of a job position. Local human resource managers use this system throughout the world to grade their managerial positions. The more senior positions, levels one to five, are ranked by human resource managers at corporate headquarters in Paris.

Once a Rhône-Poulenc manager has been earmarked for an international assignment, he or she then discusses openly with the group their preferences for the type and length of assignment. Although the importance of international experience is being strongly emphasised within the group – the 1989 annual report has a whole section on the work of the international human resources committee – Rhône-

Poulenc insists that managers are free to decline opportunities to work abroad. The company does not blacklist those who are reluctant. It simply leaves it to them to decide when would be an appropriate stage to work abroad.

On average, Rhône-Poulenc managers stay five years in each assignment, a time-span which the group feels is about right for both the business and the manager to reap the full benefits of the arrangement. It argues that it takes the manager at least a year to adjust and settle into the job and one full year to disengage from the position and make plans for the next assignment or job move. A five-year span, therefore, gives the group and the individual manager 2–3 years free from disruption.

BOC has different categories of international assignees. There are the short-term assignees, whose stay abroad can be anything from a month to a year. The second category is the international assignee who is going to work abroad for anything from one to five years. Thirdly, there are permanent transferees – employees who are prepared to sell up and move abroad for good. This can sometimes result from what was originally intended to be a short-term assignment. An assignee and family can grow to enjoy the life style of the country to which they have been assigned and lose any desire to return to their own country.

Preparing for an overseas assignment

The way in which companies prepare their employees for an overseas assignment – and monitor their progress – can be critical to the success of the exercise. The main methods used by the companies in the Ashridge survey are listed in Table 8.1 (see page 166). Some firms with large numbers of expatriate managers have set up specialist units to administer and brief managers going on foreign assignments. Obviously, as one firm pointed out, one of the best preparations for the assignees is previous work-related familiarity with a country. This company usually offers international postings to people whose previous role has brought them into contact with a specific country through either visiting, selling, marketing or some other supervisory role.

However, there appear to be few hard and fast rules about the best

Table 8.1 **Preparing managers for international postings**
(% of respondents ranking an activity as among the five most important methods in their organisation)

	%
Arranging for managers to visit host country	79
Language training for managers	73
Briefing by host country managers	67
In-house general management course	44
Cross-cultural training for managers	42
Cross-cultural training for family	38
General management course at business school	29
Language training for family	23
Training in negotiating within business norms of host country	17

Source: The Ashridge survey, 1989–90.

ways of preparing, training and monitoring international assignees. In a number of firms, a system of best practice has emerged as a result of comparing notes with other international companies faced with similar problems.

The prime purpose of providing preparatory training for international assignees and their families is to reduce the culture shock by familiarising them with local customs, particularly those that are at wide variance with home country practices. Whenever possible, companies like International Distillers and Vintners and BOC send international assignees on specialist courses, such as those run by the Centre for International Briefing at Farnham Castle in the UK. But often there is insufficient time for such in-depth preparation. The assignee is too busy winding up current job commitments and settling family and personal issues prior to departure.

When someone from BOC is being posted to a greenfield site – a location where no BOC international assignee has previously been – the preparation is more intense. BOC makes learning the local language a condition of working abroad, but this is not always necessary or practical.

"We find that most people will want to learn the local language because of the frustration of not being able to make yourself understood. But a lesson we learned to our cost is that it is sometimes better to wait until international assignees have arrived in the assignment country before putting them through language training. The first people we sent to Taiwan were put through an intensive Mandarin course for five days. When they got to Taiwan they found they couldn't use it because of the local dialect!"

Companies like Rhône-Poulenc, IDV and BOC try to limit the culture shock involved in an international assignment by sending managers and their spouses on a pre-assignment visit of about a week to the designated overseas location. This gives them an opportunity to meet future colleagues and explore local housing, schooling and other facilities. "One assignee came back from a pre-assignment visit and said the country wasn't as bad as we had painted it. I think that's good. It's wrong to tell people it's wonderful when they go out there and find it's not. We try to be as honest as possible."

The Japanese success rate

Some countries seem to be better than others at preparing their managers for overseas assignments. The relatively high failure rate of American expatriates has been attributed to the inadequate level of preparation available. Japanese expatriates, by contrast, seem to be more successful because more effort goes into preparing them for culture shock and all the other disorienting experiences associated with working in an alien environment.

A study of large US multinational corporations by two American consultants, F.T. Murray and Alice Haller Murray,[3] revealed that 10–40 per cent of their overseas assignees had to be recalled or dismissed because of poor performance. Only a quarter of the companies reported a failure rate of below 10 per cent. A comparable survey of 35 Japanese companies, however, revealed that 86 per cent reported a failure rate of less than 10 per cent.

Japan's higher success rate is attributed to the preparatory training through which they put their international assignees. The US consultants discovered that Japanese companies normally make overseas assignments at least a year before actual departure. During that year, the assignees study the culture, customs, and ways of doing business in the assigned country. Generally, they learn the language as well. Japanese companies go out of their way to:

- Equip international assignees with the inter-cultural skills necessary to maintain a high level of performance in a different and demanding environment.
- Minimise the personal stress that results from encountering unanticipated situations and strains.
- Reduce the feeling of alienation from the company that inevitably accompanies foreign assignments.
- Ease the readjustment of both employees and their families upon their return to Japan.

Japanese companies recognise the importance of their international assignees acquiring what F.T. and Alice Murray call "effectiveness" and "coping" skills.[4] Effectiveness skills empower the expatriate to translate his (rarely her) managerial and technical competences into the new environment, reshaping them to fit a different set of relations with subordinates, business associates and customers. Coping skills enable the expatriate and his family to feel at ease in a foreign environment. Unless these skills are acquired, "culture fatigue" can set in very quickly and sap the expatriate's energy.

Some companies are admittedly sceptical about inter-cultural training prior to an overseas posting. Pepsi-Cola International is one of these. In the past, the company relied on "career internationals" to run its overseas operations, people who particularly wanted to work abroad and who were often self-selecting. As a result, the company developed no special policy to prepare people for overseas assignments. Although it is more concerned than it used to be about giving international assignees some preparatory cross-cultural orientation, its director of human resources admits that he sees the value of such training as limited: "The most important thing in your mind is 'What do I have to do to make this business work?' Understanding how to get a bottling line to work or how to get distribution in Thailand is more important than knowing whether or not I should show you the bottom of my feet." (It is said that showing the soles of your feet is offensive in certain cultures.)

Catering for the spouse

There is considerable evidence to suggest that the inability of a manager's spouse to adapt to a new environment is one of the main causes of failure in overseas jobs. For this reason, managers at Rhône-Poulenc are quizzed very carefully, together with their spouses, to check whether there are any mixed feelings about going abroad. If any reservations are detected, the company has no hesitation in cancelling or postponing the move.

Prior to an overseas posting, Unilever managers are all sent, together with their spouses, on a one-week course about the country of their assignment. It is surprising how few other companies give priority to preparing the family as a whole for the culture shock of living and working abroad. The Ashridge survey (see Table 8.1 on page 166) reveals that the firms that give cross-cultural awareness training to managers frequently make it available to the family as well. On the other hand, language training for family members has a much lower priority than for the managers.

Few companies give as much attention to this area as SAS. The Swedish airline has set up an internal consultancy unit, run by Lena Ahlström, which specialises in cross-cultural education. Among the training programmes that SAS Intercultural Communication (SAS ICC) runs for both its own staff and those from other Scandinavian companies are "foreign assignment seminars". The seminars recognise that a foreign assignment is very often a family affair and that it is important that all family members are prepared.

> "After an initial honeymoon period with the new country, the family begins to find many annoying or frustrating things. That's when the real test begins. Suddenly all the networks that have supported the family at home are radically changed. The many small details that were taken care of so easily in the home country become major tasks to carry out in the new environment. It is all these simple everyday factors that people are confronted with that constitute the culture shock."

The three-day foreign assignment seminars prepare the entire family for their new life abroad. The first day focuses on inter-cultural communication and provides people with tools that help them to understand their own reactions and how they are perceived by others. On the second day participants meet specialists who give briefings on cultural background, politics, trade and industry, salaries and the standard of living. The briefings also cover language, religion, etiquette, sex roles, social relations and business life conditions. Participants meet a family that has recently returned from the country concerned.

The third day includes expert briefings on the moving process – taxes, insurance, health care and personal safety. Advice on planning for the family's eventual return is provided. All SAS staff who are assigned abroad now undergo such a programme, although SAS itself only accounts for 20 per cent of the consultancy's turnover.

SAS ICC also offers tailored seminars for outside clients. These include internationalisation seminars in which people travelling abroad are helped to learn the art of "gainful co-operation" with people from different cultures and countries. In addition, SAS ICC runs seminars on Scandinavia for companies from other countries. Outside clients include other Scandinavian firms such as ABB Asea Brown Boveri, Electrolux, Pharmacia, Skandia International, SKF and Volvo. The consultancy unit also has clients from the USA and France.

BOC, too, likes to involve an employee's entire family in the briefing prior to an overseas assignment. "It doesn't simply involve the person who's employed by the company – it's the whole family. The employee will have his work and he's got the support of the company to a lesser or greater degree than he had at home. For the spouse and children it can be difficult and we tend to underestimate that."

Dual career problems

As we saw in Chapter 5, an international assignment that threatens to disrupt the career of a spouse is one of the most common dilemmas for companies that want to send people abroad.

> "You're not just moving one person, you've got to find employment for two. That's even more difficult." (Johnson & Johnson)

"It is extremely difficult to get a work permit for the spouse and only in a few instances have we managed to find some sort of work possibility. Handling this difficulty will be one of the main issues for the future – companies must know how to resolve the problem." (Rhône-Poulenc)

"Because there are some places – the USA is one of them – where it is impossible to get a work permit for the spouse initially, he or she (and it is usually the wife because the majority of BOC employees are male) is prepared to give up or defer a career. So we have to look for other options – is there some training the wife would like to undertake while she is there?" (BOC)

In some cases, it may be possible to approach other international groups to see if they have a job opening for the spouse or "trailing partner" in the country of assignment. And it is sometimes the husband, rather than the wife, who is required to make a career adjustment. This will increasingly be a problem in the future.

Unilever gives considerable attention to the dual career problem along with other constraints on international assignments, such as the reluctance to disrupt children's education. It tries to avoid being dogmatic in its approach by handling the problem on a case-by-case basis. It has found that the main issue in dual career problems is not money but that the spouse, not unnaturally, regards his or her career as important.

The company will sometimes try to help the spouse find a job in the Unilever operation in the new country and the company's informal networks can be particularly helpful in this respect. Tony Vineall, Unilever's deputy director of personnel responsible for worldwide management development, emphasises that dealing with such issues can be very time-consuming as they are not easily delegated and will often need to be arranged at a senior level.

The companies surveyed by Ashridge view the dual career issue as a problem that will assume increasing significance. Dealing with it sensitively and providing relocation counselling inevitably adds to the costs of international management development, especially in terms of the time that senior human resource staff may have to spend on individual cases. If it reduces resentment and frustration and cuts the expatriate failure rate, however, the most enlightened international firms are likely to regard it as money well spent.

Mentoring and godfathering

Preparing international assignees for an overseas posting is only part of the story. Continuing attention is needed to the way in which the manager learns from international experience. Some companies support the maxim that "managers develop managers". They try to capitalise on the local knowledge of older, more experienced managers by appointing a younger person as an assistant department manager or as a "number two" in a country operation. In one Belgian firm, for example, an assignee is given a job as an assistant to the local manager with a specific task, such as financial control. Another company tries to assist the learning process of young assignees new to a job abroad by "pairing" them for a period of time with an experienced manager in the subsidiary.

A high proportion of companies that Ashridge has surveyed and interviewed emphasise the importance of maintaining head office links with the managers once they are actually in the post abroad so that they do not feel isolated, and of reassuring them about their future career development. Rhône-Poulenc has introduced a "godfather" scheme precisely for this purpose. Once one of its expatriates has moved abroad he or she is assigned a mentor at head office, someone with whom to keep in regular contact and who helps them consider their next career step once the assignment comes to an end. Expatriates are obliged to return to base each year to talk to their mentor, who may be a human resources specialist, a line manager or someone who has extensive experience and knowledge of the group.

At Rhône-Poulenc's headquarters in France the godfathering system is based around managers who tend to be over 50 years old, have a senior position and are approaching retirement. These company doyens are technically highly skilled, are good communicators and, most importantly, tend to have extensive contacts within the group. There are approximately 25 "godfathers" or *cadres responsables* within France, each of whom will be in contact with 200–300 managers at any one time.

Although Rhône-Poulenc is convinced the French system works well, it has not made any attempt to impose it on its subsidiaries in other countries. It has given each national business the freedom to set up a "godfathering" system which most suits its particular culture; in some countries, for example, the line manager adopts the role.

Unilever provides "contact managers" in each country of assignment to act as facilitators and help expatriates. Contact managers are people who are well versed in such areas as schooling, taxation and local regulations, and who can help to sort out the host of small problems that people encounter when taking up a new job abroad. They provide the focal point for people entering or leaving the country as expatriates. The company regularly brings these contact managers together for an exchange of views.

BOC's head office monitors its international assignees discreetly. The business units both in the home and the assignment countries monitor progress themselves, but "by keeping tabs we make sure various things happen without being seen to interfere. If things are going well, we don't hear from assignees. We have assignees whose files are very thin and we have others that take up half a drawer."

International Distillers & Vintners also tends to adopt a hands-off approach to assignments once they are up and running. Linda Clayton keeps in touch with assignees and makes international visits once or twice a year. However, IDV tries to maintain a low-profile contact between the placement company and the head office to avoid causing any disruption. Individuals can contact head office directly but they are encouraged to talk to the placement company's personnel department. Line managers in the placement company are also encouraged to treat the assignee as they would any other member of staff and to take responsibility for their performance and development.

IDV also has a "godparenting" or mentoring scheme under which a board member keeps an eye on one assignee's development. The company started the scheme as a way of facilitating board involvement, something which it sees as crucial to the success of its cadre programme. The arrangement has been only moderately successful, however, mainly because of the problem of lack of time of board members.

International assignments and remuneration

There are of course significant discrepancies between salary scales and costs of living in different parts of the world. This is why many companies seek advice from specialist consultancies in this area. One such is the London-based firm Employment Conditions Abroad. ECA originally grew out of an informal network of companies which swopped information on expatriate pay and conditions. It now has some 50 corporate shareholders and 650 member companies worldwide. A sign of the times is that fewer than half of its members are now from the UK. Scandinavian and Dutch companies were some of the first non-British firms to join, and companies in France, Italy and Germany followed. The basic question faced by such firms is how to provide the appropriate motivation for people working abroad and at the same time maintain the appropriate degree of equity. It is important to understand what motivates the individual, but "once you have more than a handful of expatriates", says Neil McMeeking, ECA's membership and marketing manager, "you must have a philosophy. You need consistency – it cannot all be individually based. The company must make it clear where it stands in all areas concerning terms and conditions so there are no misconceptions."

Consistency and clarity will be particularly important in future. "An expatriate job used to be seen as a cornucopia, as a licence to make money. Companies used to throw money at the problem. Though some still do, many are now much more cost-conscious."

When it comes to individual compensation packages, according to David Orr, ECA's director of information services, there are three important points to bear in mind: perception, control and presentation. The manager and his or her family must *perceive* the package to be fair and equitable. The company must be in *control* of what is happening. And the package must be *presented* in a way that is logical and rational. Orr emphasises that equity does not mean equality; it means that people must perceive that they are being treated fairly and that the company is consistent in the way it compensates its employees. On the other hand, there must be a degree of flexibility within the overall framework. For example, where children's schooling is concerned, if there is no suitable school available locally, other arrangements have to be made.

There are two main approaches to expatriate compensation. The "build-up" method takes the expatriate's equivalent home salary and adjusts it according to cost-of-living indices and exhange rates for the country to which the person is being transferred. The "host country" system compensates people according to local markets. It is important to have a reference point for control but there is no perfect system. The build-up approach is more logical and precise, makes the link to home-based salary and is consistent from country to country. However, it has no link to local conditions. The local market approach may be more appropriate for smaller companies or for employees going to higher pay countries such as those in continental Europe and the USA. The danger is, however, that by the time various foreign service allowances have been added to the base salary, it does not relate to salaries in either the home country or the local operation.

> "We use a build-up method when determining remuneration which starts with the home country base salary. To this we add various allowances, including cost-of-living differentials. The principle is that assignees don't lose out financially by taking up an assignment. What most international companies try not to do is to over-compensate, which makes it difficult to bring people home. Moving people from higher-paid to lower-paid countries is very expensive. This results in cases where an assignee earns more than his or her manager, but it's accepted because it is known that it is only for a limited time." (BOC)

Who pays?

It is important that the home and host country profit centres have a clear understanding about which side is responsible for the various expenses involved in an overseas assignment. Who, for instance, should be responsible for removal costs, pre-assignment visits and language courses? If an assignee is being paid more than a local national, who should pay the difference? Where an assignment arises from a request from a local subsidiary, there is a strong argument to suggest that the subsidiary should foot the bill. But when the transfer is for corporate purposes, it is reasonable to assume that head office will cover the costs.

Such an understanding is especially necessary when management development is part of the reason for a transfer. Under its cadre programme, which has a long-term development aim, IDV's head office shares the cost of an international assignment with the placement company. The operating company pays the equivalent cost of hiring a local person; head office pays any additional costs. The basis on which these decisions are made is IDV's international assignment policy which sets remuneration standards and formulae on such things as housing and foreign service premiums.

> "I am not sure that any other way of funding assignments would work. It would be very difficult to persuade businesses to take on a higher-priced person when they are only getting someone to do the job. We can argue that they are getting someone of high quality, but I doubt if that would persuade them to take on the substantial costs of the assignments."

While it is important that every assignment is professionally managed, there is no single formula that is suitable for every company. The sophisticated systems set up by some large multinational companies may not be appropriate for smaller firms with only a few employees based abroad. Clearly, expatriate remuneration is a minefield and it is highly advisable for companies to start thinking about the issue early in the process of internationalisation.

"Companies moving into the area of expatriate remuneration for the first time can get it terribly wrong. If you start out by being generous, it is very hard to stop." Setting precedents can often result in claims for upward adjustment of salaries and allowances which may eventually be expensive to buy out. Talking to a specialist consultancy early on can help a company to focus on the issues involved. The consultants will give invaluable advice on the following subjects: taxation; calculating cost-of-living differentials; dealing with social security at home and abroad; legal requirements abroad; facilities in other countries such as accommodation, motoring, schooling, sports and social clubs; and what to do about devaluation and inflation. They may also produce reports on individual countries and provide briefings.

Handling the re-entry phase

The amount of thought given to planning the assignment must be equalled by attention to what happens when the assignee returns home. "Culture change on going abroad is matched by culture change coming back, not only for the manager but for the family too," points out ECA's McMeeking.

Around 50 per cent of companies in the Ashridge survey admitted to difficulties in re-absorbing international assignees when they return from abroad (See Table 5.1 on page 103). Rhône-Poulenc considers re-entry to be the most difficult aspect of managing expatriates and confirms that it needs to be handled with as much care as the assignment itself. "The expatriate's return must be well planned. The key to handling this is ensuring that the group acknowledges that the expatriate has done well abroad. If we are not able to offer this individual some form of career advancement after he or she returns, our policy cannot be valid."

But while it is important that expatriate managers should understand the likely sequel to their job abroad, it is unwise, as Unilever warns, to promise them a particular job. The way managers' re-entry expectations are handled is a key aspect of the management of expatriation, in Unilever's view. When managers are assigned abroad they are usually told which product area in the home country they are most likely to return to. Sometimes they will be told which job they are likely to go to next. Guarantees are not possible, but it means that "somebody has to be paying attention". Unilever can only attract the necessary flow of candidates for jobs abroad if they are given reasonable certainty of re-absorption and further career progress.

Unilever is concerned, however, to ensure that the system remains flexible. To guarantee that certain jobs will be available on re-entry is far too constricting and far too complicated to achieve in a rapidly changing world. An undertaking is merely given, therefore, that expatriates will be able to go back to a job at a certain level and that it will probably be in a particular company.

When Unilever managers are working abroad they are reviewed on the basis of the latest performance appraisal in both countries. So when succession plans are drawn up in both countries, they are included in the planning process for both. Expatriates are expected, when on leave, to visit their home personnel manager to keep in touch. Unilever also believes that it is paramount to the image of its expatriate service that people are not seen to lose out on important job opportunities in their home country. If such an opportunity arises prior to the date when someone is due to return home, careful consideration is sometimes given to an early repatriation.

Looking after the welfare of expatriates and their families demands a large logistical effort. Unilever's Vineall emphasises that "all the traditional 'folksy' personnel activities are still important, but at a much more complicated level, because people are leading more complicated lives". As soon as organisations start to move people around internationally these activities come to assume a very high, almost strategic, profile.

French hotels group Accor tries to alleviate the re-entry problem by confining overseas assignments for its high-flyers to an average of three years. If the stay abroad is allowed to last any longer, the group feels there is a danger of a manager becoming "over-adapted" to the foreign environment – sometimes known as "going native". If they desire it, Accor managers can have two assignments in succession before returning to work in their home country. Accor is particularly anxious not to create a permanent group of expatriates, which would only benefit a small cadre of managers.

According to Ann Howland of BOC, most international assignees do not seem to experience too much difficulty in returning to their own environment after a spell abroad. But for a minority there are difficulties. "We have developed a small group of people who find it very difficult to settle down again and they will go out on more than one international assignment. If they go out on two or more, it becomes increasingly difficult to find jobs back home for them because it is felt they are going to be off again in a short while."

Once assignees from International Distillers & Vintners return permanently to their home countries, the period of "direct intervention" by the central personnel function comes to an end. Thereafter, the individual's career development is handled in the usual manner by local bosses and personnel staff, although head office might intervene in cases of special need. In Japan, for example, IDV has just started a two-year training scheme for one of its joint ventures in order to help it to recruit high-quality managers. The joint venture is a small company and so lacks "the clout" to compete for Japanese high-flyers, who normally prefer to work for bigger organisations which can provide broader experience and a long-term career span. IDV has introduced a scheme whereby each year staff are taken one at a time from the joint venture, given intensive language training and sent on several international assignments. The first assignee recently moved to a Canadian company in Toronto for a year, to be followed by a second year in the USA or the UK.

An important reason for paying attention to the re-entry process is that the company should be able to exploit the learning that the manager has acquired while abroad. "As well as the transfer of know-how abroad," said a German company in the Ashridge survey, "the aim is to make use of acquired knowledge at home, so reintegration of the manager on his or her return must be assured." Because of this, the company is concerned about the sequence of postings. "It is generally recognised that such assurance decreases after six years. Consequently, another overseas posting must be preceded by a job at home."

However, few organisations give much thought to capturing the learning that takes place on international assignments. NEC, in Japan, is a rare example of an organisation that encourages returning managers to document their experiences of dealing with other cultures for the benefit of managers that follow them. Companies in general could do a lot more to secure managers' recently gained knowledge of living conditions, contacts, markets, customs, cultures, governments and other valuable information about the international scene.

The rewards of sound policies

Companies that think through their strategy for managing and monitoring international assignments appear to be reaping positive results. Rhône-Poulenc, for example, believes its policies work well. The one or two failures it has seen have mainly been due to the family's inability to adjust. But it is convinced that this difficulty will subside now that couples have the opportunity to look over the country of assignment prior to taking up an appointment. "In ten years to my knowledge we've only had one person return without finishing an assignment because the family couldn't settle. We've had assignments that have ended ahead of time, but there have been sound business reasons for these. I think one in ten years is not a bad record."

But the most credible endorsement of the wisdom of a sound expatriate strategy comes from the international assignees themselves. BOC's Warren Garth is convinced that his experiences of living and working in Papua New Guinea as a financial controller have:

> "allowed me to gain exposure to issues in which I would not normally be involved within a similar job in Australia. Managing in a developing country requires you to develop skills over and above those required to manage an organisation in a developed country. You increase your technical ability because you get 'hands-on' experience of all the issues confronting a company. You develop your ability to cope with stress through both work and environmental pressures."

* * * *

International experience does not by itself guarantee an international outlook in managers, nor does it automatically develop the organisation's international spirit. Taking up a management post abroad and coping with the transition involved is difficult for even the most able of managers and the most stable of families. Companies ignore these problems at their peril because the costs of failure to both the individual and the organisation can be great. It is clear that, if international assignments are to be managed effectively, companies must invest considerably in each stage of the process. When international assignments are professionally managed by a caring organisation, the benefits for both individuals and organisation are likely to be substantial.

References

1 "International assignments on an upward trend", *BOC Management Magazine*, no. 21, pp. 7-19.
2 G. Hubbard, "How to combat culture shock", *Management Today,* September 1986, pp. 62-65.
3 F.T. Murray and A.H. Murray, "SRM forum: Global managers for global businesses", *Sloan Management Review*, Winter 1986.
4 F.T. Murray and A.H. Murray, *op. cit.*

APPENDIX 1

HOW TO BE MORE INTERNATIONAL

As a result of what we have learnt from the companies in this book, we suggest that the aspiring international manager should think in terms of development in three areas:

- global thinking and expertise
- global links and networks
- global leadership and values

The checklist which follows sets out objectives under these three main headings.

CHECKLIST FOR INTERNATIONAL MANAGERS

1. Global thinking and expertise
- Broaden your understanding of the global business environment. A book and article list (see references at the end of each chapter) should be backed by the daily and weekly internationally oriented newspapers and magazines, particularly:
  The Economist
  Financial Times
  International Management
  International Herald Tribune
  Le Monde
  Die Welt
  Frankfurter Allgemeine
  La Stampa
- Make yourself a global expert on your own industry. Understand its world standard of competition and find out what the

world competition is doing. How does your company's mission relate to this? Read the appropriate trade journals, including foreign-language publications; you can use one of the commercial intelligence services that monitor these. Attend conferences and seminars whenever possible.
- Seek out the best practices in your own industry and specialisation and consider whether you can adopt them. There is no substitute for seeing for yourself. If your company has no travelling seminars (like Fiat), chambers of commerce, trade associations and so on arrange study tours.

2. Global links and networks
- Understand your company's informal networks around the world. Seize every opportunity to forge cross-border links. Management development programmes are among the best opportunities.
- Tap into networks outside the company. Alumni associations are useful. So is the European Women's Management Development Network (men can join). Conference contacts are often valuable.

3. Global leadership and values
- Learn anything you can about cultural differences and their impact on management style; negotiation; communication and team working. You do not need to be a total expert on every aspect of the countries in which you do business. You do need to know enough about the local environment to allow it to modify your approach.
- Understand your own cutural roots and motivation.
- Improve your knowledge of other languages.
- Understand your own ethical standpoint.
- Take a short, intensive international management course at a leading business school.

— APPENDIX 2 —

PROFILE OF AN INTERNATIONAL MANAGER

Name:	Rich, Patrick Jean-Jacques
Born:	1931, Alsace, France
Educated:	Strasbourg; political science, European studies, law
	Harvard; economics (Fulbright scholar)
Languages:	French, English, German, Spanish, Italian, Portuguese
Jobs held:	1959–86, Alcan (project analyst Canada, finance director Guinea, managing director Italy, GM Latin America)
	1986–90, MD and CEO of SGS, Geneva
	1991– CEO of BOC Group

A few real international managers do exist, and Patrick Rich is one of them. Since beginning his career he has lived for only 18 months in his native France, where his childhood in German-occupied Alsace gave him an early taste of political and cultural upheaval. It also gave him two languages. He added English, which he speaks with no trace of a French accent, and later three more European languages.

Patrick Rich believes his languages have been a major advantage.

"In Latin America, for example, my wife and I had Latin American friends because we spoke Portuguese and Spanish. Other managers stayed enclosed in expatriate ghettos. They have helped in dealing with local bureaucracy, and in general business communication.

"You get a much closer nuance and feel for what is going on, particularly in negotiations. It is also valuable for communicating with your own staff and with your customers; being able to write an internal memo in the local language. It says to people that this parent company understands and respects us."

After military service, he joined Alcan in Canada as a project analyst, rising steadily through senior management jobs around the world, including Africa, Latin America, the UK, Spain, Italy and Switzerland. He had taken charge of Alcan's operations in Europe, Africa and the Middle East when he moved to SGS, the Geneva-based services multinational in 1986, and from where he was appointed BOC chief executive in 1991. His experience and adaptability illustrate the preconditions for the international manager identified in this book. A former colleague at Alcan called him a "modern Renaissance man":

> "He has an extremely wide range of experience and interests ... He looks for openness and integrity almost beyond anything else. He doesn't only want to talk about work with his managers ... He wants to know who he is dealing with as well as what they know about the business and how good their judgement is. He likes people to participate in the fullest way they can ... His decision-making process is collegiate rather than consensus – he insists that everyone around him shall have their say, but he makes the decision."

Decision-making is one of the key elements that Rich focuses on when defining internationalisation. Is a job oriented towards national or international goals ? "You don't have international managers just for the beauty of it." Assignments which are international involve:

> "analysing, planning and taking action with regard to the trade-offs between different countries and regions; understanding such things as the international manufacture and flow of components; making international alliances. (This) requires an understanding of the background of each country ... and making decisions in a competitive mode."

A second key element is the personal one; partnerships, handling cultural differences, working in consortia. With these two definitions he lists common factors found in successful international managers:

- great adaptability
- the ability to function within different cultural backgrounds, without insisting that one thing is better than another

- having been exposed to some pretty severe "knocking and testing" at an early stage through exposure to different cultures. This shakes them and makes them understand that there are many different, legitimate ways of looking at life.
- a know-how base which comes from exposure to several different national scenes and also assignments at head office, such as regional marketing director.

A highly formative experience for him was being made Alcan's regional director for Latin America. This was the first time he encountered the need to make the kind of trade-offs between different countries that he sees as the essence of international management. He had to understand national motivations and work out the investment and export patterns that he wanted. He was also involved in the details of persuading his own board of what he wanted to do. This leads him to suggest two important factors in the development of internationalism – geographical exposure, to break down the tendency to make parochial judgements, and some alternating experience between staff and line positions. At the centre, "You are always surprised at how little multinationalism prevails out there in the company." His own career is a good example of the line/staff job mix; his experience at Alcan's head office taught him about the international production and trading of bauxite and hence about international trade, taxation and the different levels of bureaucracy worldwide. In Guinea he was plunged into the nitty-gritty of an overseas assignment at the Boké mining project; the next four jobs were "skills-building exercises" in different countries, and the fifth was definitely multinational, dealing in Spain with the merger of the Alcan local operation with the Spanish firm Endasa. In Italy, next, he managed the Alcan partnership, and then went to Latin America where he put together the Trombetas bauxite project.

At this stage of his career he also joined the boards of several outside companies, a move which he suggests accelerates international development.

Despite his awareness of cultural differences, he does not believe his own operating style differs between countries. His management approach consists of a mixture of respect and dispassionate analysis:

> "Basically, people wherever they are want to do a good job and to have self-respect. Once you connect to the cultural base, you can then cope in an objective fashion."

There will be variations; for example, in some countries you may be approached for bribes, a practice which Rich refused to succumb to during his time in Latin America.

> "If you are the best company you will not lose by refusing to give bribes. There is a difference between bribes and facilitating payments, however. The latter are paid to get things which are legitimate. But you do not pay a bribe to gain an unfair advantage or bypass legal requirements."

Rich would like to see every foreman with international perspectives, but he has to accept that it is not practical to provide everyone with international exposure. He believes selection for this experience should start early, homing in on the potential high-flyers. Not all of these will be open to internationalism. Some people say they would like an international life but cannot cope with the reality. Identifying potential international managers is a trial and error process. Short assignments will reveal whether people can function effectively in an international environment, and at country manager level:

> "You want people who have a true multinational mentality. You also want to be able to put in non-nationals as well as nationals. You don't want to appoint locals who will spend their whole career in that country. They must be people with a high potential for international transfer.

Talent can however only be developed with the help of planning and the appropriate training. He recommends the young manager with international ambitions to:

> "Speak loud and clear about your own aspirations. If you want international movement it is up to you to make sure that people know it. Otherwise, all too often the people who are reluctant to move get transferred, and the people who are keen to transfer abroad are not."

Patrick Rich has taken over the chief executive's job at BOC from Richard Giordano, and will also succeed him as chairman in 1992. He sees this role in a company like BOC as having three main aspects.

1. The CEO has to have the skill to manage an organisation that is becoming more multi-polar. A global company has to be able to function at the local level and has to be decentralised with entrepreneurial, responsive local management. At the same time, it needs an international competitive platform and an international reservoir of skills. If the local company runs into problems, the corporation then has resources to bring to its assistance. The parent group provides central expertise to deal with global customers; maintains constant quality throughout the organisation; manages technology; and administers cash flow.
2. The CEO also has to be concerned with the global investment pattern and the trade-offs between investments in, say, South America or South-East Asia. This has to be based on a world view.
3. The CEO should be responsible for ensuring that the necessary human resources are being developed.

One of the problems facing any CEO of a global company is persuading highly independent managers to move in the same direction. Rich's solution will be to encourage networking that cuts across hierarchies and country barriers. He wants a corporate style in which people find it natural to solve problems across borders. BOC's Group Electronic Mail Service (GEMS) will also help. He intends to reinforce what he calls "stringers" – common values that bind an organisation together in such areas as ethics, safety codes, occupational health, training, environment, and planning and budgeting systems.

Rich does a lot of reading of business publications from various countries. He also says he does a lot of listening, but all this gives impressions only, which must be shored up with local visits. He says he cannot emphasise visiting enough, in order to keep up to date. He is an expert on the Latin American scene, yet:

> "Today I would have to approach it as if I were starting afresh. There is nothing more dangerous than being culturally akin, because it lulls you into a false confidence. You must keep up to date all the time."

He looks back on his international career to date with a high degree of satisfaction. It has given him a lot;

> "At Alcan I was able in effect to change companies without changing company. Each new job brought new challenges, but I did not have to reestablish my credibility each time. When you change job within a company your past achievements come with you."

He has been lucky in a family that enjoys international mobility as much as he does. His wife Louise, a Canadian, moved to Guinea with him 15 days after they were married, and his family has accompanied him on every job move. Each time they have followed what he calls a "survival course", involving social integration and getting to know local people quickly. His two sons and a daughter have been able to follow a French education wherever they have lived. He disapproves of the wedge many executives drive between work and family life.

> "I do not put work in one compartment of my life, family in another, music or sailing or skiing in another. These are all consuming involvements and activities that I give all my personality to. People I work with closely would probably describe me very much the same way as my family would. I have never understood why so many people undergo a kind of Jekyll and Hyde personality change on the way to the office ... apart from any other consideration, it means the business is not benefiting from the energy and intellect of people's whole personalities."

One of the lessons he has learnt from his international management career is that life can be fun as well as hard work – "and the secret is to have them both together".

INDEX

ABB 43, 170
Aburdene, Patricia 14
Accor
  business strategy 66-7
  corporate values 49-50
  international assignments 159-60, 161-2, 177
  international management 54-5
  management development 57, 118-19
  management training centre 151
  networks 61
  recruitment 129-30
action learning, General Electric 145-51
Adler, Nancy J. 75-7, 82, 83
Ahlström, Lena 169
Alcan 184, 185, 188
Alitalia, strategic alliances 19
Allen, Keith 134-6
ambiguity, coping with 45, 82
American Graduate School of International Management 154
Angus, Sir Michael 37-8, 65, 67
Ashridge Management College 155, 156

Babson College, International Management Internship Program 154-5
Bampfylde, Saxton 133
Barnevik, Percy 43
Bartlett, Christopher 26, 27, 28, 33
Baughman, James 48, 71, 145, 148
Bell, Daniel 14
best practices 146, 151
Blain, Roland 112, 128-9
BOC Group 187
  information technology in 59-60
  international assignments 160-1, 163, 165, 166-7, 170, 171, 173, 178, 180
  management culture 63-4
  matrix structure 35-6
  networks 84
Booz Allen & Hamilton 11-12
Bradford, David 86
British Petroleum 25, 39, 94
bureaucracy 30, 31, 32
Büring, Volker 49, 50, 54-5, 61, 118
business, best practices 146, 151
Business Management Course, GE 149-50
business partnerships 18-20
business planning cycles 39
business priorities, international 16-22
business schools, role in management development 153-7

cadre programme, IDV 113-16
capacity curves 120
career planning
  checklist 121-2
  international managers 107-21
Carlzon, Jan 19-20

central authority, balance with local autonomy 24-5
centralisation
  Accor 118-19
  and management development 98-100
  Unilever 37
Centre de Perfectionnement des Affaires, Paris 155
Centre for International Briefing 166
Citicorp 13
Clayton, Linda 113, 114
Clifford Chance
  corporate culture 52
  international management 55
  international operations 12-13
  overseas offices 39
co-option, decision-making through 27, 33
Cohen, Allan 86
Colgate-Palmolive 37
collectivism, national culture 45
communications
  ability 90
  corporate values 48-9
  globalisation 14
  international companies 25
  international managers 93
companies
  global 26
  integrated networks 26-7
  international strategies 26-8
  matrix structure 34-8
  mix of models 34-41
  strategic alliances 18-20
competition, increased 16-18
computers 14
consumers 15, 29
coping skills 168
core values 46-53
corporate culture 27, 33, 35, 44
  creation 138-9
Corporate Entry Leadership Conference, GE 146-7
corporate structures, changing 24-6
costs and benefits, international management postings 102-3
Crane, John, International 40
cultural differences 44-6, 71-5, 81-4, 88, 90-1, 107, 182, 184, 185-6
culture, national see national culture
culture shock
  attitudes to change 31-2
  overseas postings 169
  stress symptoms 73
currency, metaphor for networking relationships 86

Daewoo 148
Davis, Stanley 15
Davison, Sue 139

decentralisation 37
  Accor 61, 118-19
  Electrolux 29-30
  management development 98-100
  Rhône-Poulenc 111
decision-making 27, 37-8, 89, 184
Don, Alan 69, 72, 119-20
Donegan, John 94
Dow Chemical, matrix structure 34
Dowdall, Mike 37
Drucker, Peter 14
dual-careers, spouses 170-2

education, company policies 138-53
Edwards High Vacuum, matrix structure 35-6
effectiveness skills 168
Electrolux 170
  corporate culture 138
  creating the transnational 28-32
  education programmes 140-2
  management by travelling the globe 54-5
  management development 99, 119
Electrolux International Business Leadership programme 142
Electrolux International Executive Programme 141-2
electronic mail 60
elites, creation 101
empathy, cultural adjustment 75
Employment Conditions Abroad 174, 177
engineering, simultaneous or parallel 15-16
English, as business language 62-6, 144
Ericsson
  corporate values 48-9, 52-3
  international assignments 164
  international strategy 26
  as knowledge company 40-1
  leadership model 79-81
  management development 99, 116-18
  networks 60-1
Ericsson Management Institute 152-3
Ericsson Senior Executive Programme 152-3
ethnocentricity 74-5
European Management Programme 55-6
European Social Charter 126
exchange rates, metaphor for networking relationships 86
Executive Development Course, GE 149
Experienced Manager Programme, GE 148

families, international managers 104-6, 169-70
Fanuc 148
feedback, instant 46-7
femininity, national culture 46
Fiat 62, 182
  conference system 57
  Country Briefings 144
  demands of international managers 7-91
  human resources policy 99
  internationalisation of management 66
  Presentation Techniques 144
  recruitment 131
  travelling seminars 142-4
Fiat Italian Briefing 143-4
Forbo, international management 53
Fourtou, Jean-René 35
Fulkerson, John 46-7, 62

Garth, Warren 180
General Electric 18
  action learning 145-51
  corporate culture 47-8
  global outlook 71
  management education 138
  multinational strategy 26
  recruitment 124, 128
Ghoshal, Sumantra 26, 27, 28, 33
Giordano, Richard 59, 63-4, 84-5, 187
Girolami, Sir Paul 38
Glaxo, organisational structure 38
global brains, GE 146
global companies 26, 27-8
global thinking 43-4, 71, 181-2
goals, multicultural teams 83-4
godfathers, international assignments 172-3
Grand Metropolitan 158
  bag carriers 56
  management development 112-16
Group Electronic Mail Services, BOC 60, 187
Gyllenhammar, Pehr 18-19

Harris, John 11-12
head office
  burden of 39
  as coach and co-ordinator 30
  function 84-5
Hedlund, Gunnar 33
Helsinki, University of Technology 156-7
heterarchy, organisational form 33-4, 41
Hewlett-Packard 32
hierarchical organisations 30, 39, 58
hierarchy, flat 49
Hoechst AG 130, 131
Hoechst UK
  industrial scholarship scheme 130-1
  restructuring 25
Hofstede, Geert 45, 46, 71
Holzman, Win 70, 162
Hongkong and Shanghai Banking Corporation, management development 106-8
Horton, Robert 39
Howe, Geoffrey 12, 39, 52, 55
Howland, Ann 178
human resources
  management 20-2, 111-12
  policies 99-100

Iberia 19
IBM
  recruitment 125-6, 128
  restructuring 25
  transnational role 32
ICI 25, 53, 56
Impact Programme, GE 148-9
in-house publications 57-8
individualism, national culture 45
industrial scholarship scheme, Hoechst UK 130-1
information
  dissemination in organisations 58-9
  as source of power 25-6
information networks 14
information technology 58-9
  BOC Group 59-60
innovation
  encouragement 38

INDEX 191

flow in organisations 27-8
 and multi-cultural teams 83
integrated networks, companies 26-7
inter-cultural competence 71-5, 88, 90-1, 107
inter-personal sensitivity, women 76, 77
international assignment inventory, IDV 114
international assignments 158-61
 failure rate 161, 167
 mentoring and godfathering 172-3
 preparing for 165-8
 re-entry phase 177-9
 remuneration 174-6
 rewards 179-80
 selecting assignees 161-5
 spouses 169-72
International Distillers & Vintners
 international assignments 158-9, 162, 163-4, 166, 167, 173, 176, 178-9
 management development 113-16
international learning organisation 97-107
international managers
 career planning 107-16
 characteristics 68-78
 checklist 181-2
 development 7-8
 education *see* education
 families 104-6
 Fiat experience 87-91
 leadership 78-81, 88, 90
 length of postings 103-4
 life-long learning 87
 networking skills 84-6
 Price Waterhouse study 91-3
 profile 183-8
 recruitment *see* recruitment
 shortage 21-2
 team membership skills 81-4
 travel 55-6
 women as 75-8
international organisations, management development 97-107
internationalisation 9-10, 44, 66-7, 184-5
 business priorities 16-22
 management 57
 managers 53-5
 and market change 14-16
 operating across national boundaries 11-13
 restructuring for 22
 signalling commitment to 56-8
ITT 26, 27

Japan, preparation for overseas assignments 167-8
job categorisation 164-5
Johansson, Lief 30
Johnson & Johnson 69-70
 international assignments 159, 162-3, 170
 management training centre 151-2
Jones, David 51, 54, 108

Kanter, Rosabeth Moss 18, 41-2
Kao 26, 27
Kay, David 133
Kennedy, Richard 149
Kirkbride, Paul 107

languages 62-6, 131, 132, 144, 166, 183
law, employment 126

leadership 182
 autocratic 45
 international managers 78-81, 88, 90, 146
 programmes 48, 117
learning
 cross-cultural situations 74
 international learning organisation 97-107
 life-long 87
Lester, Tom 24-5
Lewington, Chris 51-2
local autonomy, balance with central authority 24-5
Lorenz, Christopher 32

McMeeking, Neil 174, 177
management development 96
 Ericsson 52-3
 international organisations 97-107
 principles 116
 strategy 100-1
management training centres 151-3
management, internationalisation 53-5
Manager Development Course, GE 149
managers
 attitude to change 31-2
 local or expatriate 101-2
 selection for international postings 102-3
managers *see also* international managers
Manchester Business School 156
markets
 domestic and foreign 13
 new 16
 selectivity in choice of 17
 speed of change 14-16
masculinity, national culture 46
Masreliez-Steen, Gunnila 17-18
Massey Ferguson 119
matrix, in the mind 54
matrix structure, companies 34-8
Matsushita, international strategy 26
mentors, international assignments 172-3
Michigan University, Global Leadership Program 155
micro-strategy, cross-cultural learning situations 74
mind-set
 international 31-2, 43-4
 new business 41-2
moments of opportunity 146
Moran, Robert T. 74-5
multidisciplinary taskforces, product development 30
multinationals 24, 25, 26, 27-8
Murray, Alice Haller 167, 168
Murray, F.T. 167, 168
Musa, Edson 35

Naisbitt, John 14
national boundaries, operating across 11-13
national culture
 impact on organisations 44-6
 inter-cultural competence 71-5, 88, 90-1, 107
 problems in teams 81-4
NEC 62, 64-5, 179
networks 78, 182
 Accor 61
 BOC Group 84
 Ericsson 60-1
 of opportunity 58-9
 Pepsi-Cola International 62, 84
 skills 84-6
 transnationals 30-1

New Manager Development Programme, GE 147
Noel, James 145, 150
non-executive directors, recruitment 136-7

Ohmae, Kenichi 13, 18
Olivetti, recruitment 124-5
Oreffice, Paul 34
organisations
 core values 46-53
 heterarchical 33-4
Orr, David 174

parallel engineering 15-16
pay, expatriates 174-6
Peacock, Ian 130
Pearson, Richard 127
people-orientation, managers 79-80
Pepsi-Cola International
 corporate culture 46-7
 cultural differences 72, 168
 international assignments 168
 International Management Institute 151-2
 networks 62, 84
perspective, managers 80
Philips 26, 62-3, 149
power distance 45, 82
"power hug" 25-6, 28, 44
Price Waterhouse Europe 91-3
Procter & Gamble 37, 124
product cycles 15-16
product development 30
professional competence 70, 89
publications, in-house 57-8

qualifications, unwillingness to accept overseas 126

Radcliffe, Mark 40
Ratiu, Indrei 72-4
recruitment 21-2, 123-4
 barriers to cross-border 126-8
 company policies 124-33
 directors 136-7
 do's and don'ts 134-6
 senior managers 133-6
Reigo, Britt 48, 49, 53, 60-1, 117
Renault, alliance with Volvo 18-19
Rhône-Poulenc 96
 global outlook 71
 international assignments 160, 164-5, 167, 171, 172-3, 177, 179-80
 management development 99
 management mobility 110-12
 matrix structure 34-5
 recruitment 128-9
Rich, Patrick 183-8
Rigby, J. Malcolm 81-2
Rolander, Dag 33
Rosenkranz, Danny 36

SAS
 inter-cultural competence 72
 Intercultural Communication 169-70
 as service company 41
 strategic alliances 19-20
Scharp, Anders 29
self-esteem, managers 79
senior managers, recruitment 133-6
Shell
 Inter-Cultural Communication Workshop 139
 international management 53

simultaneous engineering 15-16
Singapore Airways, strategic alliances 19
single European market 9, 24, 37, 56
skills, shortage 21-2
social skills, women 75-6
Sorooshian, Tirad 125
spouses
 dual-career 170-2
 and international assignments 169-72
stability zones, coping with culture shock 73
Stanford, Naomi 91-2
Stanic, Vlad 123, 127, 132
Stopford, John 36
strategic alliances 18-20
strategic awareness, international managers 68-70
strategic business units (SBUs) 35
support staff, professional partnerships 91-2
systems architecture, BOC 59-60

talent-spotting lists 109-10
Tang, Sara 107
teachable moments 146
Tesio, Vittorio 88, 91, 143
Thunderbird 154
TI Group
 corporate culture 51-2
 restructuring 39-40
training
 Accor 50
 for international assignments 167-8
transnational corporations 26-8, 41
 creating 28-32
travel, managers 55-6
TSB Group plc 123, 127, 132
Twist, Neil 59-60

uncertainty avoidance 45, 82
Unilever 27, 62
 characteristics of managers 78-9
 corporate culture 50-1
 human resources policy 99-100
 in-house publications 58
 international assignments 160, 171, 173, 177-8
 international management 54
 internationalism 67
 language policy 65
 management development 108-10, 153
 management education 138-40
 matrix structure 36-8
 recruitment 131-2, 134
Universitätsseminar der Wirtschaft, Köln 155
universities without walls 151-3

values
 core 46-53
 shared 33
Varity
 inter-cultural competence 72
 management development 119-21
 strategic awareness 69
Vikersjö, Kurt 31, 32, 56, 142
Vineall, Tony 50-1, 79, 108, 110, 132, 171, 178
Viney, John 134, 136, 137
Volvo 18-19, 170

Wild, Alan 112, 114, 115
women, as international managers 75-8
Wriston, Walter 13